Just as You Are

Opening Your Life to the Infinite Love of God

PAUL COUTINHO

LOYOLAPRESS.
A JESUIT MINISTRY
Chicago

LOYOLA PRESS.
A JESUIT MINISTRY

3441 N. Ashland Avenue
Chicago, Illinois 60657
(800) 621-1008
www.loyolapress.com

Cover photograph: © W. Cody/CORBIS
Cover design by Paul Uhle
Interior design by Mia McGloin

Library of Congress Cataloging-in-Publication Data
Coutinho, Paul.
 Just as you are : opening your life to the infinite love of God / Paul Coutinho.
    p. cm.
  ISBN-13: 978-0-8294-2721-9
  ISBN-10: 0-8294-2721-X
  1. Spirituality. 2. Spiritual life—Christianity. I. Title.
  BV4501.3.C695 2009
  248.4'82—dc22

                                                          2008031339

First paperback printing, November 2012
paperback ISBN-13: 978-0-8294-3761-4
paperback ISBN-10: 0-8294-3761-4

Printed in the United States of America
12 13 14 15 16 17 18 BANG 10 9 8 7 6 5 4 3 2 1

To St. Ignatius of Loyola: my inspiration
and whose spiritual journey has been my pathway
to attain growing personal freedom

Contents

Part 3: Being in Love with God

Introduction: A Note to the Reader

When I wrote my previous book, *How Big Is Your God: The Freedom to Experience the Divine*, all I wanted was to share my spiritual journey and the gifts and blessings that God had showered on me. I imagined that only those who knew me through the retreats and different programs I lead would be interested in reading that book. But upon its publication I began to receive feedback from so many people around the world telling me what a difference it has made in their lives and how it has helped them in difficult and trying situations, I realized that a true spiritual experience is universal. Even though so many of my stories were from a different culture and a different time, people in this day and age and from diverse cultures have identified with those stories and experiences. I realized that in spite of my weak and imperfect self, God's gifts and blessings were meant to be shared with others.

And so, I decided to continue to do that by writing this book.

It was many years ago when I first realized that God was trying to teach me this lesson of sharing my spiritual gifts. I had joined the Jesuits soon after high school. Two years after I finished my novice training, the novice director asked me to give a retreat to the new novices. Can you imagine that? Two years after being a novice myself and here I am being asked to give an Ignatian retreat to other novices. Now, I was not a priest at the time. I told these young men that I was going to give them an Ignatian retreat. What does that mean? It means I give the retreatants a talk on some spiritual theme and then afterward meet with them individually to reflect on how God affected them in their prayer and help them discern this.

Every one of those novices came to me and shared wonderful stories about what God was doing in their lives—except one. This one Jesuit novice looked me in the eye and said, "When I heard that you were going to give this retreat, I was very angry." I asked him, "Why?" He said, "Because you are not a priest! How can *you* give a retreat?" I thought to myself that this young novice must not know that St. Ignatius, the founder of our order, gave retreats as a layperson, long before he became a priest. You don't have to be a priest, you don't have to be a nun, you don't have to be a religious to give a retreat.

But then the novice told me that he had opened his Bible and found a passage that helped him tremendously, and now he was ready to give himself fully to this retreat experience. And so I asked him, "Tell me! What was that passage that made such a radical difference?" He said, "You know the one from St. Paul, where he says, 'God uses the foolish things to confound the wise'? *That* one."

Now trust me, it took me about fifteen years to learn what God was trying to teach me through that novice. Until I was ordained, my ministry was work and *I* had to do it. I developed and used *my* gifts, *my* talents, and *my* thinking—all for the kingdom of God, of course. I did it all for God, without counting the cost, but I did it *my* way. The day I was ordained, I began to find that God put me into situations where I had to fall back on weakness and foolishness. I had to fall back on weakness and foolishness so that *God's* strength and *God's* wisdom were able to come through and affect the lives and hearts of the people I ministered to. I finally realized that I was just a channel for God to reach out to people. I continue to develop my gifts and talents but now it's to be a more effective instrument in God's hands.

So this is one of the reasons why I continue to direct retreats, give talks, and write books about deepening a relationship with God and about experiencing the Divine. It is in my *weakness* that God's strength works; it is in my *foolishness* that God's wisdom has a chance to affect peoples' lives. And it is with that kind of attitude that I am sharing this book, *Just as You Are: Opening Your Life to the Infinite Love of God.*

Another reason I want to share my journey through my speaking engagements and writing is to deepen my own spiritual gifts. I believe that those gifts and graces that we share with someone, in one form or another, are the only ones we own, and they become the platform for bigger and greater graces. Those that we do not share we tend to lose forever. St. Paul tells us that gifts and graces are given to us for the growth and development of humanity (1 Corinthians 12:7; 14:12–13). And so here I wish to share with you more of my spiritual journey, new stories, and further wisdom from saints and sages who have inspired me and others throughout the ages.

When I look at the path my life has taken, I cannot but feel a very special closeness with the Divine. This relationship has kept me adventurous in the way I live my life and gives me the freedom to make mistakes. As this relationship deepens I also experience my own identity as it is revealed in the Bible and by the many mystics. My first experience of the Bible was Psalm 8. It was my favorite song in childhood that I sang with so much devotion:

> Great is your name Lord, its majesty fills the earth. . . .
> When I see the heavens, the work of your hands,
> The moon and the stars which you arranged,
> What is man that you keep him in mind,
> Mortal man that you care for him?
> Yet you have made him little less than a god.
> With glory and honor you crowned him.
> Gave him power over the works of your hands.
> Put all things under his feet.
>
> —Psalm 8:2, 4–7 (song lyrics)

Whenever I begin to write about God or talk to people about God, somewhere in my subconscious the words of this Psalm begin to resonate. And I always try to ask myself: what kind of a relationship with God am I introducing to people? In my previous book I explored how a person can move beyond the mere practice of a religion into having a living relationship with God—how to open oneself to an ever-greater experience of the Divine. Here I am writing for the reader who wants to go even deeper—even more fully into union and communion with the Divine. To fall in love with God. To be seduced by God, to romance God, and to grow in one's love with the Divine.

Falling in love with God begins with an invitation, a Divine seduction that has an irresistible attraction. Many years ago I had a dream that I consider a landmark in my spiritual journey. In the dream, it was a gorgeous day and I was standing in front of this familiar mountain in India, Duke's Nose. I soon found myself climbing the mountain. But as I got closer I began to see someone on the very top of this mountain. I first saw the outline of a figure, and yes, it looked like Jesus. My heart skipped a beat, my eyes stayed focused, and my feet picked up a steady quick pace toward Jesus, a stately figure dressed in red with his hair moving in the wind. The sky was a rich blue and there was a gentle breeze across my face. Everything seemed so mellow and so very peaceful. I reached the top of the mountain and I looked into those loving but piercing eyes of Jesus. I was ecstatic. But he did not let me stay for long. Jesus in my dream pointed to a path in the other direction, and I soon found myself on a winding but beautiful road. I carried the image and the experience of Jesus in my heart and set out on a new quest and a new beginning.

My God does not let me build the structures on the mountain that Peter wanted to build after witnessing the Transfiguration. Every time I reach a peak in my relationship with God, my spiritual journey is directed to another winding path, to a greater height toward the Divine.

This journey is also one with challenges and obstacles: to fall in love with God is like going through a furnace, where one is purified by the fire without being consumed. You may experience misunderstanding, alienation, and pain from those who are closest to you. You may let down your family, lose your friends, and disappoint your heroes. You may begin to second-guess yourself and even feel totally lost and abandoned as God at one point or another will draw you into the desert in this journey. The desert is a place that systematically strips you of all your securities—your personal psychological defenses, the masks that you wear, your culture, your religion, and even your relationship with God. In the desert you begin to experience your true self as you are drawn closer to the original face of the Divine, a face that goes beyond images, labels, theologies, and even religion.

Being in love with the Divine is God's gift that is always available to anyone who is looking for it. We have all had a taste of Divine love and our spirits hunger for more. But then other voices muffle the unconditional gift of Divine love—voices that speak of fear, guilt, anxiety, and unworthiness.

Falling in love with God begins with an infatuation that penetrates those negative voices, and we respond to this either by being more and more attracted to the Divine or we are repulsed by the experience. We come closer or we fight to get away. In either case our focus is the Divine energy that is drawing us to itself.

The Divine seducer never gives up but continues to draw us in many different ways to a deeper union and communion with the Ultimate. But when all is said and done, the falling in love will be up to you.

So if you really have the will to experience life as one who is in love with the Divine, it will happen. If you want it, you'll find it. In fact, love will find you.

Are you willing?

Are you ready?

1

Seduced by God

1

God—an Experience

God is not a religion, not a theology, not a belief—God is an experience that takes you into the fullness of life. All experience is discovering the fullness of God, discovering the original face of the Divine, beyond all the titles and images. Through experience, I find my own identity in the Divine and see the Divine presence manifested in all of life.

We know that God—what we attempt to refer to when we use the word *God*—is always bigger than anything we can know about God and deeper than any experience that we have of the Divine. And so we ask ourselves, "Do I have a relationship with God, or do I have religion? Has my experience of God or my relationship with God changed in the last five, ten, or twenty years? Have I seen the face of the Divine?" If we cannot answer yes, then in all likelihood we know *about* God, but we don't know God. Maybe we do not have a relationship with God. We probably have a theology, or a ritual, or an idea from our parents or the church. But we do not really know God. An experience of God, on the other hand, gives us knowledge that touches our hearts and transforms our lives more and more into our divine identity. We feel more and more interconnectedness with all of life.

There is a difference between the Eastern and the Western understanding of knowledge and truth. The Western understanding of truth is a set of beliefs, a philosophy— something that you can think and know about. The Eastern understanding of truth is an experience. This experience can contradict your philosophy, can defy science, can even challenge the Scriptures, and yet, in the Eastern view, your experience is both knowledge and truth.

In Sanskrit, a classical Indian language, the word for experience is *anubhav*. It means "toward life's Essence" or "toward fullness." So experience is that which tends to make me a whole human being or a more fully human being who lives the fullness of life. The pathway to *anubhav* is *sat-cit-anand*.

Sat means "truth," but Mahatma Gandhi expressed *sat* as the Divine being and essence. In his philosophy, *satyagraha*, a word popularly translated as "nonviolence," is actually an earnest invitation to oneness in the Divine. In Gandhi's struggle with the British in India, he invited them into a relationship through our common identity in the Divine being and essence. Later he tried unsuccessfully to pass on the same belief to Hindus, Muslims, and Christians in India. During one of the worst Hindu-Muslim riots, Mahatma Gandhi went on a fast unto death. When people begged him to give up his fast, saying that they would be willing to do anything that he would suggest, Mahatma Gandhi said, "Are you a Hindu? Then go into the streets and look for a Muslim orphan child. Take this child into your home and bring it up as a good

Muslim. If you are a Muslim, then take in a Hindu orphan child and bring that child up as a good Hindu in your Muslim family." Gandhi was trying to teach people our oneness in the Divine being and essence. This is the challenge and the reality of *sat*.

Cit, "pure consciousness," is a means to attaining *sat*. *Cit* is not attained through the thinking mind or the feeling heart but through the Divine Spirit who dwells at the core of every human. Pure consciousness goes beyond the senses and perceives *sat*, the Divine being and essence in all of creation.

The sign that one has experienced *sat* is *anand*, which means "eternal bliss." It has no beginning and no end; *anand* just is and is experienced at all times, in all places, and in all circumstances. It is that peace that the world cannot give and an inner contentment that no one and nothing can take away.

And so every time we go to pray, every time we seek a deeper relationship with God, we need to have *anubhav* (the experience) of *sat-cit-anand*. Our work, our ministry, our relationships with people and even reading this book ought to bring us closer to the fullness of life.

How does one attain *anand*? By listening. This is a listening not with the thoughts of the mind, not even with the feelings of the heart, but through pure consciousness, by being present to life and allowing life to happen to us.

There is a legend about an island that existed a long time ago. On that island was a temple that had a thousand different bells that would ring with the gentleness of the breeze and the fury of the storm. The sound of these bells always brought one to a state of pure consciousness, to the core of one's being, to the experience of total peace and tranquility.

As legend has it, the island temple slowly sank into the sea over the years. But the bells never ceased to ring, and anyone who knew how to listen would hear the bells and have the same experience of *anand*.

A young man, inspired by this story, traveled many miles to an island rumored to be near the sunken temple so he could experience the bells for himself. Every day he walked to the shore to listen for the bells, but all he heard was the sound of the wind, the waves, and the many sea birds. He tried to push every sound out of his mind to focus only on the sound of the temple bells. He spent many hours a day, for many, many weeks straining to listen for the bells. But he couldn't hear them. He prayed and fasted and tried harder every day to push out all other sounds and focus only on the sound of the bells. He learned new techniques, read books, and consulted the priests on the island. None of this helped him hear the temple bells. He decided that perhaps he was not worthy of hearing the bells. And eventually, he began to believe that maybe the legend was just a good story and not really true.

On the last day of his trip, having resigned himself to his fate, he decided to go one last time to the seashore. Only this time rather than straining to hear the bells and fighting all other sounds around him, he noticed the palm trees and enjoyed the wind rustling through their leaves. He heard the sound of the waves dancing over the waters and breaking in a melody that calmed every nerve in his body. The sound of birds emptied his mind and heart of the tension he had been holding. For the first time since he came to the island, he was relaxed and happy. As he basked in this newfound tranquility he heard the tiny sound of a bell. Then more bells, and the sound grew louder and clearer, until slowly but surely he heard the beautiful ringing of the temple bells.

Falling in love with God will happen if we just let life happen to us. When we stop struggling to find God and instead allow ourselves to experience life, we will be drawn into the Divine presence and essence.

2

Involution and Evolution

I have a favorite quotation from Kabir, the great Indian mystic. He said, "I laughed when I heard the fish in the water say that it is thirsty. How can the fish in the water be *thirsty?*" Kabir continues, "But it is easier to understand fish in the water being thirsty than a human being not experiencing God. Because God is closer to a human than water is to fish."

In the Eastern tradition we talk about involution and evolution. The movement of God in our lives and what I would like to call God's seduction is part of the whole flow of the universe between involution and evolution. *Involution* is where God, the Divine, empties itself into creation. The spirit—Divine Spirit—becomes matter. *Evolution* is the process of matter finding its identity by moving back into the Spirit. We are spiritual beings, come into this human or earthly existence, looking for our identity and our authenticity as being spirit, divine, and holy. So our origin is divine, our existence is divine, and our end will be divine.

The Bible tells us in Genesis that God breathed his Divine breath into us and we became human. This means that our human condition is not something like: *The Divine is "out there," and I'm here trying to plug into the Divine.* No, I'm *in* the Divine. And, like the Jesuit poet Gerard Manley Hopkins wrote, the Divine is poured into everything: "the world is charged with the grandeur of God." Everything is charged with Divine energy. Everything is charged with the Spirit. God is right here. We just need to be able to recognize it.

We need to experience the universe coming from God, living in God, and ending in God. God is part of this whole reality, and we are part of this whole reality, and all that we need to learn is how to experience this reality. Because we're already living in what Teilhard de Chardin called the divine milieu.

There's a story that Anthony de Mello, the celebrated retreat leader, would tell about a fish that was swimming frantically from side to side in the ocean. Another fish asked, "What are you doing?" He answered, "I'm looking for the ocean." "You're in the ocean."

So what are you looking for—God? You are in God. What are you looking for—the Divine? You are in the Divine. We're all living in this Divine atmosphere, breathing this Divine love, and everything is vibrating and pulsing with the Divine life.

The problem is in our perception. We are looking at the world with a distorted vision. We are looking at the world and life not as it is, but with our prejudices, with our beliefs, with our upbringing, and with our past experiences. If we let go of all that, peel it off part by part, we will be able to see ourselves

3

Are You in Love—or Is It an Infatuation?

B eing infatuated is not the same thing as being in love. There is a difference.

When we are infatuated with someone, we have two ways of responding: we either repulse the person we are infatuated with by being mean or distant, or we manipulate the person in various ways to try to draw that person to ourselves. And we sometimes even martyr ourselves just to win the favor of our infatuation. At the same time, we want to lead this relationship *our* way, as opposed to letting ourselves be led by love. We are so obsessed by this other person that we tend to be blind to everything else. This process can be very self-destructive.

On the other hand, falling in love is letting ourselves go, letting love decide, and letting love carry us.

St. Ignatius of Loyola's initial relationship with God was one of infatuation. He was drawn to God by reading the life of Christ and the heroic lives of the great saints. He was enchanted by the life of Jesus wanting to establish a king-dom and was envious of the saints who were pillars in this kingdom. He wanted to win the admiration and love of God by outdoing the saints. He began to imitate them in their extreme ways. In his infatuated state, he was in competition with the other suitors of God. He took the lead in this rela-tionship and was trying to draw God into the relationship his way, on his terms. And Ignatius wanted this at all costs.

Infatuation is not love. In fact, infatuation can lead you to suicide because when you are infatuated, nothing that you do is good enough, and what glares as you try to purify your life is the negative. And suicide is the temptation that Ignatius had. After his spiritual reading and reflection, as his infatua-tion took root, he went through a period in which he intensely berated himself for all his past sinfulness. He didn't feel wor-thy enough for God or for this life, and he contemplated end-ing everything. All that he experienced was darkness and being abandoned by God. He was in deep spiritual desolation.

It was only when Ignatius stopped leading God his way and allowed God to take over that he had his revelation at the River Cardoner in Manresa—an experience that forever changed him, where he fell completely *in* love with God. There in this little Spanish town, Ignatius was suddenly drawn into Divine love. Now there was no competition. Now there was no definition of what the relationship should be. Now Ignatius was just in it, loving. And love drew him and freed him to be the person that God created him to be.

I, too, was infatuated with God before I fell in love with God. When I was infatuated with God, I thought I had to do many and challenging things to prove that I was in love with God and to get God's attention. I wanted to be someone who God would notice. But whatever I did, it wasn't enough. I joined the altar boys when I was twelve and traveled fifteen miles every morning to serve the first Mass. I was part of the Sodality of Our Lady and gave myself to the pious practices and social service without counting the cost.

When I joined the Jesuits, I opted for the most menial works and took up the biggest challenges. I was infatuated with God and not in love with God. The truth was I hated myself and could not love God. I remember a time when my superior asked me to take care of a companion who was in the hospital. I was by his bedside any free time I could find. Right after breakfast, I was on my bicycle racing to the hospital to make sure he had had a good night's sleep and had a good start to the new day. After lunch I was back again to see that he was comfortable. I sacrificed my leisure time and my recreation to be with him and make sure he was not alone. On the day of his surgery, the Jesuit in charge of the sick could not be present, so I stayed close to him. I nursed him, fed him, cleaned him, and bathed him—I did everything I could for him. And all this I did unconsciously for the admiration of my superiors and companions and to draw God's attention to myself.

But when my Jesuit classmate came home from the hospital, he inexplicably began to spread all kinds of negative rumors about me. I felt that I was judged unfairly, felt totally rejected, and was the laughingstock of my other companions. I was deeply hurt. But at that time I was sure that God was aware of the way I martyred myself for this companion and all for the love of God. You see, I was looking for a martyr's crown. I was expecting a great reward in heaven.

When I look back at this experience, I feel that I deserved what I got. Why? Because Jesus said we are to love our neighbors as ourselves. At that time, when I was infatuated by God, I did not love myself, and so I was incapable of loving my classmate or anyone else. All the things I did for this young man and for the rest of the world in the name of God were *acts* of love—not love. And acts of love, not love, got me what I deserved. Everything I did was to use the other person to show the rest of the world how wonderful I was—acts of love to prove to myself what a good person I was, acts of love to use others to gain a great reward in heaven. Acts of love can, therefore, cause deep depression or even make a person suicidal.

Since I did not love myself I could not love anyone else. I looked for ugliness and negativity everywhere. I was sensitive, caring, smart, and athletic and yet did not feel worthy of anyone's friendship and love. I was talented and yet thought others were better than me. I always seemed to focus on something that did not go well in my life, however small or insignificant. I was incapable of friendship, of loving, or even receiving love, because I did not love myself. In my relationship with people and even in my relationship with God, I was loving for the scraps, the crumbs, anything that would fall from the table. Whatever might satisfy me for the moment but ultimately would leave me empty, feeling degraded, resentful, and far from happy. How I craved for someone who would love me just for myself. I remember praying in one of my dark and desperate lonely moments, "Lord, take away all my talents and gifts and send me one person who will love me for myself." I cried while praying many nights, feeling alone and lonely.

And then one day in probably the lowest period of my life I discovered my mantra. It was given to me: "I'm important, I'm precious, and I have something beautiful to offer—that's me." Once I found my mantra—important, precious, and beautiful—everything changed. My whole life changed. I didn't have to prove to God who I was; I just knew. I'm important, precious, and beautiful, and not because I say it but because the Bible tells me so. God did not create trash when I was created; God made me in God's own image and likeness. I am the Divine breath (Genesis 1 and 2). And in Isaiah 43, God says, "I have called you by name: you are mine. . . . You are precious in my eyes . . . I love you. . . . I have created you for my glory." Isaiah 49 says in no unclear terms that we are so precious that God carved us on the palms of God's own hands. And Jesus assures us that we are more precious than the birds of the air and the lilies of the field. I used so many passages in the Bible to discover and assert my own personal identity. And then slowly but surely I didn't need to rely on the Bible to tell me this because I began to experience it. I experienced it again and again, and I now feel it at the core of my being—important, precious, and beautiful.

Today I don't have to prove my love for God. I don't have to do anything to be in love with God. Whatever I do is not necessary; the relationship doesn't require validation or justification. This loving relationship just is. That's the difference. I'm no longer infatuated with God, I'm in love.

So, infatuation is not love—though it can lead to love.

4

Stories of Being Seduced by God

If we focus not on ourselves but on the movement of God in our lives, we can see how falling in love with the Divine begins. Like all things, it begins with God's initiative. It begins with something I like to call God's seduction.

Jeremiah, the Brokenhearted Prophet

It seems that Jeremiah was not allowed to enjoy his youth. The Bible tells us how God broke into the life of this ancient Jew and called him to be a prophet when he was very young and minding his own business. God reveals to the youthful Jeremiah that he is loved in a special way and part of the Divine plan long before he was even born. God speaks to him, "Before I formed you in the womb I knew you, before you were born I dedicated you, a prophet to the nations I appointed you,"—and Jeremiah is seduced. At this revelation Jeremiah is love-struck and anything that he does to resist the Divine offer to this special relationship only throws him deeper into the arms of God. He complains that he is just a kid and not a gifted speaker—and God promises to put words into Jeremiah's mouth and promises to be with him at all times. The seduction deepens.

As soon as Jeremiah sets out on this Divine mission people make fun of him, he is put in prison, and at one point he is even thrown into a pit to die. He was often bitter about his experience and expressed the anger and frustration he felt. He cursed the day that he was born and wished that his mother's womb were his tomb. Here are Jeremiah's own words:

> You have seduced me, Yahweh, and I have let myself be
> seduced;
> you have overpowered me: you were the stronger.
> I am a daily laughingstock,
> everybody's butt.
> Each time I speak the word, I have to howl
> and proclaim: "Violence and ruin!"
> The word of Yahweh has meant for me
> insult, derision, all day long.
> I used to say, "I will not think about him,
> I will not speak in his name any more."
> —Jeremiah 20:7–9, Jerusalem Bible

Once again Jeremiah tries to resist God's way of drawing him into the Divine experience through this mission. But the more he struggles to resist God the more entangled he gets in the Divine web. He continues to exclaim:

> Then there seemed to be a fire burning in my heart,
> imprisoned in my bones.
> The effort to restrain it wearied me,
> I could not bear it.
> —Jeremiah 20:9, Jerusalem Bible

What does Jeremiah get in return for being in this seemingly treacherous mission? He sees himself as clay in the hands of the Divine potter, who is shaping and forming him slowly but surely into the Divine image and likeness. As he reviews his life, Jeremiah confesses and proclaims that God never abandoned him in all his trials and desperation. He has no doubt that he had a special share of Divine life and love. Jeremiah invites the rest of the world to believe and experience this tremendous love of God for us as individuals and for the whole of humanity in any and every situation of our lives.

> The LORD appears to him from afar:
> With age-old love I have loved you;
> so I have kept my mercy toward you.
> —Jeremiah 31:3

Have we sometimes felt like Jeremiah, brokenhearted? We are drawn into situations and ministries that seem beyond us and something we never would have looked for. How many have sacrificed their entire lives to take care of an ailing or aging parent or loved one? How many have given their best to the jobs and ministries they are in, sometimes at the expense of family, friends, and their own personal needs and interests?

We do the best we can to carry out what seems to be God's plan for us and yet our best does not seem good enough and we feel inadequate. When we feel punished, or mocked, or even abandoned, may we also feel the steadfast love of God drawing us into the same everlasting love that seduced, sustained, and transformed Jeremiah.

Adam and Eve, the First Seduction

In most ancient traditions and cultures the serpent is a symbol of wisdom. The book of Genesis talks about a serpent in the story of Adam and Eve, and we are told that the serpent possessed secret wisdom that no other creature had. In the story, the serpent seduces the woman, Eve, into eating the fruit from the tree of the knowledge of good and evil. The serpent proposed that it was a source of wisdom that God wanted to keep from them. It's a familiar tale, but let's challenge ourselves to look deeper.

The feminine intuition recognized that the fruit from the tree of wisdom and knowledge "was good for food, pleasing to the eyes, and desirable for gaining wisdom" (Genesis 3:6). Eve shares the fruit with the man, Adam, who eats as well. This results in our first parents becoming aware of their nakedness. And what is nakedness? After they made the decision to eat the fruit and not trust in God, nakedness was their natural state, living with no masks and no pretenses. They lived comfortably together, seeing themselves as God's own image and likeness and the Divine breath.

But the seduction of wisdom in defiance of God comes with a price. In the story, Adam and Eve make loincloths for themselves to cover their nakedness. Skins were put onto humanity's nakedness—skins that created Jews and Gentiles, slave and free, male and female. Our true selves are covered with separations, distinctions, and pretenses. Following this path of wisdom has other consequences as well; namely, judgment, punishment, alienation, and suffering not by our adversaries but at the hands of those we love most.

True wisdom, which is the gift of God, helps us see ourselves more and more as we truly are, and this knowledge of our true identity gives us a growing inner freedom. But this knowledge is also countercultural and sometimes antisocial, and it often makes those we love most and are close to very uncomfortable. To avoid being ridiculed or ostracized by others—or to avoid the chance that they, too, may be seduced—our loved ones will stay away from us or punish us and make us suffer. As God draws us in, it is not our enemies, but those we love and cherish most who resist us and alienate us. This is the paradox and the price that comes with growth in wisdom.

Yet, true wisdom continues to seduce us. It challenges us to keep seeking greater and greater wisdom, until we come to the tree of life. It is then we will experience the fullness of wisdom and find our true identity in the Divine.

It is our human destiny to be seduced by God. That's why we begin to fall in love with God in the first place, because God actually seduces us. God invites us to eat from the tree of knowledge—to have a Divine experience—and that experience shows us our nakedness or transparency. Or to put it another way, our inherent thirst and craving for the gift of the tree of life—our human desire to live fully and infinitely—creates in us restlessness with our current state, a deep, burning fire challenging us to continue seeking that deeper consciousness. We keep seeking the greater and the better, and we are drawn deeper and deeper into the Divine love.

So this is God's pattern, I believe—one of seduction. It starts right from the Bible book of Genesis; Adam and Eve were seduced and experienced themselves as the likeness and image of the Divine. And so will we if we let ourselves be seduced like Adam, like Eve, like Jeremiah.

Abraham, the Settled One Uprooted

Scripture scholars tell us that Abraham was a tribal chieftain who had everything going well in his life. He had his land, his people, his culture, and he spent his life being good and doing good, faithfully worshiping many gods. Yahweh gently came into this good life and seduced Abraham with the promise of a land for him and his descendants that would stretch as far as one can gaze to the north and south, east and west, a land flowing with milk and honey. His descendants would multiply like the stars in the sky and the sand on the seashore. He would be a blessing everywhere he went, and all the families of the earth would bless themselves by Abraham.

Abraham fell for this Divine seduction. He left the security of his land, his people, and his culture. He abandoned the many gods that he worshiped and had found comfort in all his life. He was drawn to encounter the one true God.

Abraham was infatuated by the Divine promises. But the path to the land flowing with milk and honey was through the desert. God led Abraham into the desert, and it was here that Abraham found himself stripped of all his securities. This was where Abraham was confronted with himself, where his whole life was challenged, and he was not sure whether he was going to live or die.

In his nakedness he encountered his true self and experienced God without all the comforts of Divine gifts. But once Abraham fixed his eyes and his heart on God there was no turning back. He was seduced and his infatuation kept him going as his faith in God deepened.

God now demanded of Abraham the sacrifice of his son Isaac, "the son of promise" and God's own gift. What a price! And Abraham could not refuse. He now fell in love totally and unconditionally with the Divine. The transformation from infatuation to love was complete. The Divine was the absolute, and Abraham found his identity in this absolute God. This Divine love spared Isaac and transformed Abraham into our father in faith and the father of a holy nation.

Have we not felt like Abraham at times in our personal lives? We spend our lives doing good. We follow all of God's commandments. We reach out to those in need. We sacrifice ourselves so that our families are settled and happy. And it seems that God is not satisfied. More is demanded of us. The signs of God's presence in our lives seem to be destroyed. Our faith is challenged, we feel forsaken and abandoned by God, and we find ourselves in the desert, stripped of everything except our true selves. And our relationship with God is also stripped of everything, of all labels and theologies. But we may take heart knowing that it is here that we truly encounter and fall in love with the original, absolute face of the Divine. Also, we realize that with God there is always a better than the best. When we think we have given our best to God, more is demanded of us. By the same token, when we think we have received the best from God, there are always better gifts that surprise us.

Moses, the Curious One

Moses' life can be summed up with one word: *curiosity*. When Moses was a baby and Pharaoh's daughter saw his papyrus basket floating down the river, she was curious. She looked inside and saw the baby Moses. Moved with pity at the sight, she took him into her home. Even though Moses lived in an Egyptian home he was brought up knowing he was a Jew. His heart was with his people who were in slavery at the time. He must have struggled with his identity— outwardly he was part of the Egyptian family but his heart was still with the people of God. As a grown man, he kills an Egyptian who was beating up a Jew. And then in the aftermath, when some of his own Jewish people were ready to betray him, he had to flee.

God seduced Moses by working on his curiosity. While traveling in the desert, Moses encountered a bush that was burning but not consumed by the fire. His fascination drew him closer to the bush, and then his heart was trapped. God spoke out of the bush and told Moses to take off his sandals; he was on holy ground. At this point Moses could have run away, but his curiosity got the better of him. He draws still closer and begins to converse with God.

Moses had worshiped the God of Israel up to this point in his life without really knowing who this God was. His curiosity drew him into a deeper revelation and a closer relationship with God. Now he falls in love with God whose name is "I AM." Moses was seduced by God, his infatuation drew him to the burning bush, and now he intimately converses with God and falls in love with the Divine. And he himself is burning with this Love of the Divine, without being consumed.

But this gift comes with a price. Moses is sent back to Egypt to set God's people free from the tyranny of the Pharaoh. He realizes his weakness more and more as he carries out his mission and yet cannot resist God's continual seduction. God overcomes Moses, and Moses overcomes the Pharaoh.

After he completes his mission to free Israel, Moses continues to be seduced by God, who said, "I AM is with you." Moses finally gets his people out of Egypt—and now they rise up against him. "Why did you bring us out here? We were better off in slavery and bondage than here in the desert." And faithful Moses is drawn deeper into I AM. In his total dependence on God, Moses is sucked into the very being and essence of the Divine: at Mount Sinai God draws Moses into a divine cloud and overshadows him.

Having fallen in love with God, Moses' work does not become easier. He has to deal with a stiff-necked people who refuse to be seduced as he was. And his self-doubts do not allow him to go into the Promised Land with the Israelites, but they do not stop him from drawing ever deeper into the Divine presence.

How often in our lives do we find ourselves in situations that are on fire with the love and the presence of the Divine but never consumed. It attracts our curiosity. Do we run away? Or are we ready to remove our sandals, empty ourselves of our selfish egos, and allow the Divine energy and presence to take us into itself. If we stay and follow, like Moses, our weakness does not stop us from taking on the strongest people and the most challenging situations. Instead, it is through our weakness that God works. It is in our weakness that we, like Moses, find our identity in the Divine. In the process we are taken into the cloud and overshadowed by the Divine presence. We have fallen in love with the Divine and there is no turning back.

Mary, the Blessed One Who Believed

The Gospel of Luke tells us how at the Annunciation Mary is seduced by promises brought by the angel Gabriel. "Hail, full of grace! God has found favor with you. Will you bear God in your life?" Mary seems infatuated by this greeting and cannot run away. She asks the angel how this would happen. She would be overshadowed by God and her son would be Divine. She is told that her cousin Elizabeth is pregnant even in her old age; God's seduction gives Mary tangible signs that the angel's message is true. Mary's response is not a yes or a no, but a surrender to life experience: "Let life happen to me according to God's word." Then when Mary allows herself into this love relationship, the angel leaves her. She feels totally abandoned with the Mosaic law ringing loud in her ears: either a quiet rejection by Joseph her future husband or a public stoning to death.

Mary is love-struck and runs to the hill country to her cousin Elizabeth, both to help her in the time of her pregnancy and to seek confirmation and support on her new journey with God. As soon as Mary arrives, John the Baptist leaps in his mother's womb while Elizabeth pays Mary the best compliment when she exclaims, "Blessed are you who believed." This belief in the ways of the Divine keep purifying Mary all her life. She returns to her home, and of course Joseph is ready to dissolve their engagement and send her away quietly. In the face of rejection from someone so close to her, Mary is forced to abandon herself to the Divine.

This rejection continues as she travels with Joseph to Bethlehem, where one door after another is slammed in her face. There is no room for her to lodge and no proper place for her to give birth to her firstborn. She was told that her son would rule the earth but is not even provided with a decent place to give birth.

After Jesus is born, God continues to seduce Mary, first through the shepherds and then through the Magi. The shepherds tell Mary about the angels who appeared to them in the middle of the night telling them about Jesus the Messiah, and the Magi reveal to Mary their experience of following a star that led them to the manger. She understands none of this but ponders all of it in her heart while she has to pick up her little baby and flee to Egypt. God probably became more real to Mary as she finds no secure place except in the heart of God or God in her heart.

Jesus grows and his relationship with the social and the religious leaders of his time throws Mary more and more into the arms of the Divine. When he is just twelve, he stays behind in the temple as his parents travel on unaware, and when Mary complains about it, all he says is, "Did you not know that I must be about my Father's business?" Mary does not understand any of this. He grows up and he spends his time with those condemned by the society and religion of his day. His life and preaching is against the religious powers that lead his people.

Mary arrives with Jesus' relatives, who think he has gone crazy and want to bring him back home (Mark 3:20, 31–35).

Jesus continues to live a life that is an expression of his Divine seduction and Divine identity, and this brings him to the cross. Mary does not understand any of this but keeps living her first response: Let life happen to me according to God's word. Good things happen in the life of Jesus, and Mary is there taking in the good without clinging to any of it; painful things happen, and Mary hears the crowds scream for the death of her son—"Crucify him! Crucify him!"—and she feels the pain but does not cling to it. She is now *standing* at the foot of the cross. Her mother's heart is broken, but in her romance with God her divine spirit gives her the strength to take it all in with the sure hope of the resurrection of her son.

Mary is now one who has attained total union with the Divine and experiences inner freedom and the fullness of life. She finds her identity in the Divine, and like her son Jesus, lives in that truth.

Don't we at times in our lives feel like Mary—bewildered, rejected, with no secure place or thing to cling to, save our belief in God's love? Haven't we all been broken down at one time or another by life's uncompromising events or the judgmental actions of others? And how many of us have felt the sting of death claiming someone we love too soon? But we find our inner strength when we have the courage to say like Mary, "Let life happen to me according to God's word. I believe." When we cease to cling to our own expectations and conclusions and begin to flow with life, then we begin to let God's life live in us.

God's Pattern

So from these stories we can see this is God's pattern, seduction. But it is seduction of a different kind. To be seduced by God is actually an invitation to die—it is an invitation to let go and an invitation to give up. God is calling us, wooing us, into a new relationship, and for this relationship to deepen, our old selves and our identity as we know it must die. What you might be thinking now is: "Maybe I've made a mistake reading this book. Why would I—why would anyone—want to fall in love like *that?*"

Because, to not allow oneself to be seduced by God is to forgo the incalculable gift of experiencing Divine life. It is to pass up what it means to truly be human—to refuse to be seduced by God is to forgo knowing your real identity. Not letting go, not giving up, and not dying to self leads to misery. We merely exist; we do not live. God is seducing us so we can live our life fully, live our life happily, live the abundance and the fullness of life. Jesus said in the Gospel of John, "I came so that they might have life and have it more abundantly" (10:10).

So we ought to ask ourselves some important questions:

- "When have I experienced God's seductive invitation in my life?"
- "What was it that first enticed me into a deeper personal relationship with God?"
- "How have I responded?"
- "How did this response affect my personal life?"

When you are being seduced by God, there is this burning desire inside of you: *I want to, but I am afraid. I try to pull back, but I can't.* You can't pull back because God is that kind of seducer. And once you start falling in love with God, once God crosses your path, it's very difficult to stay away. How long can one resist God's power? God is more powerful than you and me, and if given a little chance, God will take everything. God will take everything we currently cling to in order to give us back everything that is our right—peace that the world cannot give, freedom that no one can grant, inner joy that no one and nothing can take away.

Our first step is to open ourselves to experience. To be seduced by God, to respond like Adam and Eve, Jeremiah, Moses, and Mary, our attitude must be a burning desire to experience wholeness, to experience fullness, to experience ultimate truth. And yielding to this seduction is the first sign that we are falling in love with God.

5

You Need a Burning Desire

Spirituality is meant for people who want to follow their dreams and desires. To fully experience life in relationship with God, you need to be a dreamer. If you do not have a dream, you are hopeless for the spiritual life. You will not experience God and God will not impose on you.

Your desires are there—God puts those there. Your most heartfelt desires and dreams are God's plan for your life, your purpose—although this may not look like what you think it will at the outset.

When I was finishing high school, my first desire was to be a sailor. It was certainly not to meet people or even to see new places, but to experience the challenge and mystery of the open waters. I grew up on the beaches of the Arabian Sea and spent many hours and many days of my younger life on the beaches of Bombay and Goa. I would spend time thinking about the deeper aspects and questions of life, and sometimes I just let the mystery of the high seas flow into me.

Even though I did not follow the path of a sailor, the spirit of the high seas continues to live in me even today in different aspects of my life. In my spiritual life I want to launch out into the deeper waters more and more. My inner spirit always finds itself beyond sacred boundaries and seeking new horizons. I want to develop the gifts and talents that God has given me as much as I can. Life continues to be an adventure and a continual quest into the unknown.

In my early years as a Jesuit I developed a longing to live, work, and die in Africa. I placed my desire before three of my superiors at different times, and none of them thought that I should leave India. Even though I will probably never be sent to work in Africa it has affected all my preparation for my future and my present ministries. I developed a zeal and generosity in my ministry, as if I were in Africa. If I did not have Africa on my horizon, I would probably have lived a very mediocre life of quiet desperation and at worst felt that I had a meaningless existence.

This reminds me of a young woman who wanted to be a doctor but whose parents would not send her to medical school. They had sent her brother, who was a year older than she was, to medical school, and now they could not afford to send her. She felt that she was being discriminated against because she was a girl and was younger. Although this was true, I told her that given her family's financial situation she would not be able to go to medical school. But then I asked her why she wanted to be a doctor, and she said she wanted to be of service to the sick. I helped her understand that a nurse is often of more service to a sick person in a hospital than a doctor. A doctor may see a patient for a short time every day, but the nurse is with the patient for many hours every day for as long as the person is in the hospital. A nurse connects with the family more than the doctor does. A nurse in a very real way is at the hub of the services available to the patient in a hospital. As the young woman listened, she felt a rainbow form in her heart while her tears flowed through her compassionate eyes. She went on to become a great nurse and then to teach in a nursing college, passing on her values and mission of ministry of service to hundreds of nurses who will work in different hospitals in different parts of the world. Her nurses find a personal dignity, and their patients have more compassionate help.

I imagine that even if our desires are sometimes not very rational, it is better than someone without any desires at all. I remember an older religious priest who once told me that he felt God was calling him to be a bishop, and he was wondering what he should do. Of course, no one who goes out to tell people that God wants them to be appointed a bishop would be made bishop by the church, much less a priest from an order. But this priest was sincere in his relationship with God and so I asked him what he thought God wanted him to do as bishop, and he talked about how he would be pastoral both to other priests and to the laity. I said that he could begin to do this every day until God made his desire a reality, or maybe this desire would never become a reality, but the effect of such a desire on his day-to-day actions would make this world a better place and would make him a happier and a more fulfilled person.

In each of us our most heartfelt desire is a sign of our purpose, a sign of the principle and foundation of our lives. I begin to determine my purpose in life by my heartfelt dreams and desires. How can I best deepen my union and communion with God by following these dreams and desires? This is spiritual discernment—which I believe is finding the harmony of what I want and what God wants. Ultimately, you do what you want because as you grow in your relationship with God, what you want is what God wants, and what God wants is what you want. My sincere desire is God's will for me.

Following your desire is to follow your bliss—your *anand*—not your happiness. Happiness is different. Happiness is transitory and situational. Bliss is that which doesn't have a beginning and doesn't have an end, that which always is. It is just there. When you're in love with God, you follow your bliss.

At the same time, you have to be careful about your dreams and desires because God usually grants them. Maybe you've heard about the man God "offered three wishes to." And the man said, "Oh, my God, what should I wish for?" So he says, "Put me on a beautiful island." And God said, "Done." Suddenly, the man was standing on this beautiful, magical island. Then God appeared beside him and asked the man for his second wish. So the man said, "Can you make this island like a James Bond set? I want to feel like James Bond." And he was dreaming about all the women he would have and the cars and the many complicated gadgets and all of that. God said, "Done. Third wish?" For his last wish the man said, "Since you insist, God, here's my final wish: could you send me the perfect woman to be with me on this island?" And while his mind took off on many a romantic fantasy, God sent the perfect woman—Mother Teresa.

So it is best to be thoughtful when it comes to your desires and dreams. But it is better to have great desires, even wrong desires, than no desires at all.

6

A Sincere Decision Is Better Than the Right Decision

It is better to be sincere and later realize that one is wrong than to be right but dishonest. This is true in life, and especially true in the spiritual life. So along with the necessity of dreams and desires, in our relationship with the Divine a sincere decision is always better than the right decision.

What is a sincere decision? Take the example of St. Ignatius again. For many, many years Ignatius believed that God wanted him to go to Jerusalem and spend his life there, assimilating the life and spirit of Jesus Christ in prayerful contemplation of the places where Jesus lived and also helping others to experience the gifts and graces that Jesus offered us. Ignatius made a firm decision to go after many mystical and foundational experiences. He went to Jerusalem but was forced to leave by the Franciscans who were guardians of the Holy Land. They did not want Ignatius to be taken captive by the Moors, who would demand a ransom and deprive him of all the vital sacraments of the church. The Franciscans were protective of Ignatius's soul and eternal salvation—so they forced him to leave.

Ignatius vowed to return to Jerusalem. Years later he convinced a close group of companions that they should follow him there, too, but as Ignatius's life unfolded he finally realized that that was not where God wanted him to be. He was supposed to be someplace else—in Rome leading and directing the fledging Jesuit order. That was God's will for him; that was where the Spirit again and again guided him. Not to Jerusalem as he had dreamed of. But Ignatius was sincere. He followed the will of the God he so deeply loved. And his sincerity ultimately got him to a place better than his dream of Jerusalem, the place he was *really* supposed to be—lost more and more in the being and essence of God.

God may put desires in our hearts that are never fulfilled but will affect the quality of life that we live. Ignatius never went to Jerusalem again, but he lived in Rome as if he were in Jerusalem, with the same zeal, with the same inspiration. And therefore he was so effective in all that he did.

Or take this example of sincerity: Two sons are answering their father, who is asking them to do something for him that they both find distasteful. One son grumbles in disagreement and the other says, "Yes, yes, I will do it"—but never does. The latter son was doing the right thing. The good thing. What was the sincere thing to do? To grumble and say a spontaneous and blunt no, and maybe later to go and do it?

Dishonesty is doing something because I think you want me to or because everybody else is doing it or because the church says to do it or because someone tells me God says to do it, but I don't really believe that it is what *I* am called to do. My true self doesn't agree. But if I do it anyway, then although that may be a right decision, it is also an insincere decision. Internally I am reinforcing a dishonest and an unhappy life. And that is a sad situation to be in.

There was a time when Anthony de Mello was promoting the Gandhian way of living. People dressed and lived like Gandhiji. De Mello asked me what I thought of this, and I said that it was a great thing. And he asked me why I was not following the Gandhian way of dressing and eating, and I told him then that I was not called to do every good thing in this world. I am a great admirer of Mahatma Gandhi and his experiment with truth, but I do not feel called to be literal in following him.

I remember an old man who was always forthright and expressed his opinion freely. One time after the Sunday liturgy he went up to the celebrant and told him that his homilies were boring and really bad. He was sincere. But his wife who felt embarrassed and wanted to say what was politically correct blurted out, "Please do not listen to my husband, Father. He just repeats what everyone else is saying."

You need to be honest in your relationship with God. And that starts with being honest with yourself. Take teenagers who grow up and leave their parents' household. Often they break from the faith and conventions of their upbringing to chart their own course and eventually experience God, but in a different way. They have found *their* path, and they are fine. They may not always have done what is right, but they were sincere. Most often, in the end they are okay.

One time, there was a mother who asked me to pray for her child who had lost his faith. In my ministry I find that this is a typical worry that many parents have. So I asked the mother, "How old is this child?" And she said, "He is forty-five years old." The next thing I asked was, "Is this child of yours generous?" And she said, "Oh yes! He and his wife are the most generous people in the family. But they don't go to church." And I continued, "Do you think he has God in his life?" She responded with a firm, "Yes. But what about the sacraments?" Finally I said, "I believe that this child of yours is close to God. And you need not worry about his salvation." The mother sighed with relief saying, "Thank you. I feel a big burden that I have been carrying for many years has been lifted." How often I want to tell mothers that the ones they may need to worry about are those children who go to church but aren't generous of heart and don't care about the rest of the world.

We need to remember the sad story of the boy Samuel. The Scriptures tell us that he spent all his time in the sanctuary of the temple. He performed all the rituals and practices and served the temple well—he did everything that was good. But when God called out to him, he did not know the voice of God. Samuel would run to the high priest, Eli, wondering if it was the priest that had called him. And what about the high priest, Eli? He, too, had spent his whole life in the temple, and yet when God called, even he did not know God. Eli knew the rituals and did everything that was good, but God was not in his life and thus was unknown to him. This story comes with a warning: the longer we spend time in the temple, the greater the danger of not knowing God and losing our relationship with the Divine. No wonder Jesus said openly that the tax collector and other sinners were rushing into the kingdom of God, while the Scribes and the Pharisees, who were the religious people of his time, were not—or at least were not at the front of the line. So just because our children go to church does not mean they have a relationship with God and are growing in love.

In the spiritual life, each one of us needs to sincerely look into our hearts and ask, What is the sincere decision for me, or the sincere orientation of my life? The right thing to do is what we are already doing—we all are doing so many right things. But is that the sincere thing?

Finding your sincerity is not easy. Whenever I give a retreat to priests and nuns in India, I make them go through the discernment process again about being in a religious order to find out whether God really wanted them in the first place—and it is disturbing. It is frightening for them. Here they are, fifty or sixty years old, and some of these priests and nuns have decided, "No, God did not really call me." And it's not because they are bad nuns or bad priests—no, they are the good ones. They are being sincere. Then there are others who simply think, "God wanted me because I do not know what to do if he did not." And most are afraid of finding out. An old sister once said to me, "Please do not ask me to think about my calling again. I am too old to find work and too ashamed to beg. Let me die being a sister." So finding your sincerity can be scary. Some will have to say to themselves, "I am fifty years old and when I joined this order, I was sincere. But join-ing might not have been the right thing to do. And for all the wrong reasons I have stayed here. Now do I have the courage to say, 'I have to go'? When I made the decision in the first place, it was a sincere one—but when I look back, it was not the right one. Do I have the courage to be sincere again now?"

The same thing can happen with the decision to get married. If you made the decision to get married wrongly, at least now you can look at it sincerely, honestly, with yourself and with God. This is not easy. You have to look at the sincerity of what you did and let God determine the flow and direction of the relationship. That may mean getting out of a bad relationship, or it may mean acknowledging wrong choices and making the best of what you have.

Now if I realize that my sincere decision of long ago was not the right one, I can at least admit it and try to make the best of the life that I am living rather than pretend that all is well and live a life of quiet desperation and unhappiness.

In the classical Indian tradition, when a couple had fulfilled all their obligations to their children and their married life, the husband and wife went into the forest to find the deeper meaning of life and to enjoy and celebrate life more fully—and after a period of time there they separated. Each one went their own way because there was more to life than marriage. The same with the priesthood. There was more to life than the priesthood. So after a priest had served sincerely in the temple—served with all his heart—then he would just disappear into the Himalayas, into the mountains, into the forest. He went out because there was more to life than just serving in the temple.

7

Obstacles to Love: Sin

There are obstacles to being in love with God. These obstacles inhibit our ability to surrender ourselves to God's deeper and deeper seduction. The two main obstacles are sin and attachment. Let's look at the first one—sin.

Sin is always in the context of my relationship with God. Every time my relationship with God deepens I have a greater sense of my own sinfulness. When Moses experienced God in a deeper way at the burning bush, he recognized and accepted his limitations and his sinfulness. He could not trust God's choice of him to lead the people of Israel, and he realized his weakness and lack of confidence in himself. And in this very experience he was also given the gift of his fundamental consolation, what I call his root grace. His God, who was the God of Abraham, Isaac, and Jacob, is now I AM. And I AM will be with the self-doubting Moses, always.

When Peter encountered God in the miraculous catch of fish, he threw himself facedown and pleaded with Jesus to depart from him for he was a sinful man. Here in the presence of God, Peter was again deeply aware of his weakness and limitations. And he receives from Jesus his mission of being "a fisher of men." Peter, who was until then called Simon, is also given his true identity, *Cephas*, which translates as Peter and means "the rock" on which Jesus will later build his church. To Peter, Jesus takes on the role of Master; Jesus will lead the emotional and often rash Peter step by step along the way, just like a teacher leads a little student. Peter will be strengthened and refined into one so steady and mature that he can lead the church—his root sin transformed into his root grace. His root grace is finding his center, his inspiration, and his power in Jesus, his Master.

At the miraculous catch of fish, Jesus had advised Peter to cast his nets farther out, resulting in a haul so great that the nets couldn't contain it. This initial command of Jesus to launch out into the deep continued every step of Peter's spiritual journey, with him freeing himself of his sinfulness, his sense of inadequacy and insecurity, each time he yielded and followed.

When Zacchaeus, the tax collector and a public sinner, accepted Jesus into his house to share a meal, he was overwhelmed. He experienced the freedom that comes from meeting the God who loves him unconditionally. Through this encounter, Zacchaeus could acknowledge the fact that he was a sinner and at the same time begin to recognize who he really was through God's unconditional love. As a sign that he had experienced the Divine, Zacchaeus offered half his wealth to the poor and with the other half he repaid anyone whom he had cheated four times over. Zacchaeus systematically freed himself of his sinful baggage to become a true child of the covenant that God made to humanity through Abraham: "I shall be your God and you shall be my people."

The Samaritan woman at Jacob's well is introduced to God who is spirit and truth. This was a woman who had been trying to find meaning and love in multiple relationships. Jesus reveals to her the source of life-giving water: The source of true meaning and love is not in any temple or on a mountaintop—that which she has been seeking through multiple relationships is found deep within her. After this discovery, she changes her entire life and now becomes Jesus' publicity person: "Come see a man who told me everything I have done. Could he possibly be the Messiah?" At her experience at the well, this woman recognized herself as she truly was—a child of the Divine. She was no longer the outcast Samaritan in a Jewish land or a second-rate person in society because she was a woman. Jesus helped her realize her personal dignity and find her true identity in the depth of her being.

Then again, the woman who had been caught in an act of adultery was waiting to be stoned to death and Jesus reached out to her saying, "Has no one condemned you? Neither do I condemn you. Go, and from now on do not sin any more." In saying "do not sin any more," Jesus confirms her spiritual and divine identity and tells her never to forget who she is—a child of God.

Similarly, Mary Magdalene never looked back to her past. Mary Magdalene's passion for life was the need to love and the need to be loved. Until she met Jesus, she fulfilled her passion in destructive relationships. Once she channeled this energy into her relationship with God in Jesus, she became one of the greatest lovers of the New Testament. This transformation led her to live the fullness of life. She maintained her inner freedom, both in the pain of the Passion and the glory of the Resurrection. With Mary the mother of Jesus, she stood at the foot of the cross. Rooted in God's love, this woman was also the first to experience the Resurrection and announce the risen Christ to the apostles. The freedom and power of the Resurrection was her root grace, the meaning and message of her life.

When Paul experienced God on the road to Damascus, he was a totally changed person. He changed his identity from Saul, who found his personal identity in keeping the Mosaic law, to Paul, who was driven by the love of God. With his experience at Damascus, Paul made great strides on his way to the Divine: "Just one thing: forgetting what lies behind but straining forward to what lies ahead, I continue my pursuit toward the goal, the prize of God's upward calling, in Christ Jesus." Paul now found his personal identity through the Divine who lived in him. Paul was taken up to the mystical heights ("'What eye has not seen, and ear has not heard, and what has not entered the human heart, what God has prepared for those who love him,' this God has revealed to us through the Spirit" [1 Corinthians 2:9]) and this while he was still weak ("that I might not become too elated, a thorn in the flesh was given to me, an angel of Satan, to beat me, to keep me from being too elated. Three times I begged the Lord about this, that it might leave me" [2 Corinthians 12:7–8]). In this experience Paul found his root grace: "but [God] said to me, 'My grace is sufficient for you, for power is made perfect in weakness.' I will rather boast most gladly of my weaknesses, in order that the power of Christ may dwell with me . . . for when I am weak I am strong" (2 Corinthians 12:9–10). Paul's weakness became the source of experiencing God's presence and power in his life.

We, too, will truly experience the deepening of our relationship with God in our sinfulness and weakness. If we let sin cloud our deepest dreams and desires, then we believe only in our sinfulness and weakness instead of in God's promises and Divine love. Here sin is an obstacle to being in love. But if instead we allow ourselves to experience the Divine in our weakness, in our sinfulness, this too becomes a channel for God's presence in our lives and the realization of the Divine.

8

Through Our Root Sin to Our Root Grace

In our experience and relationship with the Divine we come to recognize our true personal identity. As we are drawn deeper into a relationship with God we recognize more and more our own Divine identity. We recognize that we are God's image and likeness or even the Divine breath. When we lose sight of this identity, then we live in sin, because when we do not see God's goodness—the Divine image and likeness—in us, we will not be able to see it in anyone else or in the rest of creation. On the other hand, when we are aware of the Divine presence in the whole of God's creation, then we will treat every creature with the reverence it deserves.

Jesus himself said that we should love our neighbor as we love ourselves—we must love ourselves to be able to share our love with others.

In many traditions, such as my own Catholic tradition, it is common to instead focus on one's own sinfulness. Now this is where people often get confused. God is not interested

in the list of your sins. God is not waiting to indict you. All
God cares about is *you*. Like the father of the prodigal son,
God is waiting for us to show up so God can show off. So
when you look into your sin, what you really want to know is
what is keeping you from accepting this tremendous love of
God for you. *Why* do you sin?

When I look deep into my sinfulness, I realize that I
have just one sin. Each person has one root sin, and all of his
or her other sins are an expression of that root sin. But amaz-
ingly, when we find our root sin, we will also find our root
grace. Our root grace is the same energy of our root sin channeled in a positive direction. The root sin and the root grace
are linked.

For example, St. Ignatius's root sin was vainglory.
When he was young, Ignatius's whole life revolved around
attempts to gain glory for himself. This was his root sin, and
from it came all his other destructive behaviors. What was
his root grace? *Ad majorem Dei gloriam* (AMDG)—"For the
ever greater glory of God." After his conversion experience,
Ignatius understood what real glory was and AMDG became
his motto. So he took this energy, which had exhibited itself
in a negative way, and through grace he changed the focus
from himself to the Divine.

Psychologist Carl Jung says that we all have a shadow—
a dark side of our personalities—made of repressed aspects
of our conscious self, things we do not wish to accept within
ourselves. Root sin is like our shadow. You can't get rid of your
shadow. You can't get rid of your root sin. Vainglory would
only die when Ignatius died. Jung says that the only way to
deal with the shadow is to romance the shadow, to dance with

the shadow, to make the shadow work for you. So you take the energy of vainglory and direct it toward God. Everything Ignatius did was now for the ever greater glory of God.

Or take the example of the good thief who was crucified alongside Jesus. What was his root sin? He was a *thief*; he stole. And what did he do on the cross? He stole heaven. As he is being crucified, this man uses the last moments of what was ostensibly a disreputable life to ask Jesus to remember him when Jesus enters his heavenly kingdom. This thief used what he knew best, his root sin, and he channeled that energy into his root grace. That is, he stole heaven. Jesus says, "Today you will be with me in Paradise."

This is what it means to look deep into the dynamics of our sinfulness. It is not to go through a list—because that list, by the way, will be the same list that you will still have five minutes before you are dying. The sins that we commit and confess as teenagers are the same sins we still struggle with for the rest of our lives; we never get rid of them. We look for and attend seminars, we read spiritual books, we learn theology, and we get different and sometimes more adult or theological names for our same sins. But when we begin to understand why we sin, we can channel that energy into our root grace. So as a person falls ever more into love with God, this is another thing that happens: the person tends not to focus so much on his or her sin as much as focus on his or her root grace.

For the person who is in love with God, the sacrament of confession is not a confession of sinfulness, but an opportunity to celebrate the experience of God's love. In the act of confession the energy of sin is transformed. Confession, I like

9

Another Obstacle to Love: Attachment

Every human being is connected to other human beings, to all of creation, and to life itself. But sometimes this connection becomes an attachment and affects our freedom and inhibits our ability to make sincere decisions. From my personal experience and dealings with people in spiritual direction, I have concluded that we are attached to those people, places, and things that we have not fully enjoyed.

First, let me explain what attachment is and how it works. When one of our normal everyday connections to someone or something gets out of balance, we have formed an attachment. Attachments blur our vision from seeing life as it really is, and instead we see a distorted reality based on what we think we want or need, or the way we think things should be according to our personal judgments or expectations. Our vision will continue to be defective when we relate with people and things because of what we can get out of them for ourselves rather than loving for the sake of loving.

When we form attachments, we get possessive, envious, and jealous, and we tend to lose our inner peace and tranquility. We see things not as they are but as we are. All attachments aren't necessarily sinful, but if left unchecked long enough, they will inhibit our personal freedom, limit our spiritual growth, and ultimately lead to sin.

The easiest way to overcome any attachment that is not sinful is to learn to appreciate it and see it as a gift from God, to be able to enjoy it and then watch it lose its hold on us. We can only love when we are not attached. It is then that we will be freer to experience the presence, power, and essence of the Divine in every creature.

If you have fully enjoyed something, you want other people to have it—you want to share it. If this thing that you fully and thoroughly enjoyed is taken away, you say, "I enjoyed it. I am grateful for the joy it brought into my life, and I hope that the one who might have it now will enjoy it as much." And you let it go. Or you might express your gratitude to this thing or person for helping you get in touch with your inner source of happiness and you say a fond good-bye. You may experience the pain of loss but without suffering the loss of your self.

We can only relate to someone if we enjoy that person and are not attached. This applies to our relationship with God, too. I was once at a cloistered convent, and one of the older sisters was telling me that the goal of her life was to cling to God and I said, "You better let go of God or else you will choke God to death." Our attachment to God will prevent us from growing or even relating with God. When we are so closely attached to God, we cannot see God as God is.

We do not even see ourselves in this relationship. It is a clinging that destroys God and us and the relationship. The more we cling to a handful of sand the more it slips through our fingers. The only way to hold the sand is to let it be. We can then watch it and enjoy it, and it will stay there forever. As soon as we clench our fist to possess the sand, we begin to lose it. It is the same with all our relationships. It is the same with God.

10

Two Misunderstood Spiritual Tools

True spirituality seems to be based on a bedrock of mortification and abnegation—two "scary" words that seem to jar today's modern sensibility to accentuate everything pleasurable in life. But I believe these words have been misunderstood and given negative connotations. What is actually achieved through these two very effective means is the ability to live and enjoy life to the fullest. They are processes for overcoming our attachments, and they enable our capacity to experience God and become lost in the Divine.

I use the terms *mortification* and *abnegation* to mean the intentional and internal process through which we identify and get rid of everything that is self-centered and selfish in our lives, thereby freeing ourselves from crippling attachments. Mortification and abnegation give us the freedom to love persons, places, and things for themselves—not just for what they can give us. We grow as human beings in proportion to getting rid of selfish interest. Through this self-emptying process we put on the attitude of God, who is emptied out into all of creation and is present and available to everyone. For one who is mortified, it becomes easy to encounter and experience God in all things.

I am reminded here of one of the Buddhist ways of explaining the Christian Trinity. The Father created the world by emptying his divinity into all of creation, the Son redeemed the world through *kenosis*, or self-emptying, and it is through the outpouring of the Holy Spirit that the world is sanctified. The purpose of our lives is to become a part of this self-emptying dynamic to become one with the Divine Trinity. This is what mortification and abnegation is all about.

Applying abnegation and mortification in our lives might mean, for example, being more present to others, emptying our mind of negative or selfish thoughts, and abolishing the compulsive behavior and excess in our lives. For instance, to get rid of negative or selfish thoughts, it would be helpful if we immediately turned our minds from these thoughts onto something positive. Also we should be conscious of when these negative or selfish thoughts occur so that later we can reflect on what was happening in our mind to prompt them and then do something about it. This would be a way to overwrite the negative thinking with a positive and realistic alternative.

So mortification and abnegation are not meant to make us miserable; they are meant to make us happy and free. They help us to seek pure enjoyment. They help us experience bliss, happiness, and contentment without selfishness. They have nothing to do with being masochists or punishing ourselves. They are about using the power we all have within ourselves to clear the path so that we can enjoy our lives to the fullest. They help us get out of the way of the things that trip us up, that snag us, that weigh us down, that make us less free.

A mortified person does not need long hours of prayer to unite him or her with God. Be suspicious if we find ourselves spending too much time in prayer because soon we will be looking for good feelings rather than the source of all goodness—God. Very surely those who spend long hours in prayer will find themselves, not God, and this spiritual pride will be reflected in the way they relate to God and the rest of the world. We become like the Pharisee who thanked God that he was not like the rest of humanity. Without mortification and abnegation, we more easily become obstructions to the union and harmony of the world and the groups we belong to.

On the other hand, when John the Baptist proclaimed that Jesus "must increase" and he "must decrease," he did not mean that he would disappear into nothingness so that Jesus could take center stage. The Baptist means he would find his true identity as he let himself become more and more one with Jesus and his mission. John prepared the way for Jesus to bring in the kingdom of God. This preparation helped in the fulfillment of Jesus' mission. In fact, John the apostle writes in his first letter that "when [God] is revealed, we shall be like him, for we shall see [God] as [God] is"(1 John 3:2). So as God is revealed to us, we will also realize our true identity in the Divine. Through our mortification and abnegation we will be so transparent that we will reflect the Divine without losing any of our true selves. This is the true effect of mortification and abnegation.

Thus, just as it is with root sin, our attachments can be transformed into opportunities to experience grace: the more we are able to let go of our self-imposed limits and attachments, the more we become who we truly are in the Divine.

11

What's Your Focus— Your Rock or Your Garden?

The traditional way of overcoming sin and attachment is by sheer willpower. But can we overcome anything by willpower? We can keep it in check but we cannot really overcome it. And as I have said, we do not really change—our root sin and our shadow will be with us when we die.

We look at the Gospels and, for our consolation, see that no one really changes. Look at Peter. He was a poor fisherman and very impulsive. After the resurrection of Jesus, when Peter was on Lake Tiberius, he announced that he was going fishing. Now, everyone knew that Peter did not usually catch fish. But Thomas, a community-driven person, agreed to go with him and convinced the other disciples, too. We have seen this trait in Thomas before, when Jesus wanted to go to Jerusalem to wake Lazarus from the dead. Going to Jerusalem at that time was for Jesus like walking into a death trap. When nothing could change Jesus' mind, Thomas exclaimed, "We will all go and die with you."

And yet, Thomas was also the one who wanted to put his finger and hand into the side of Jesus before he would believe that Jesus had truly risen. This doubting Thomas did not change, even at the very last moment when Jesus appeared to the Eleven before leaving this earth for the last time. This happened in Galilee where Jesus had asked them to go. When they saw him, they bowed down and worshiped him even though some of them doubted. Thomas was with them.

Now when Thomas and the other apostles were with Peter fishing all night, Jesus appeared at the shore early in the morning, but they did not recognize him. Jesus called out to them and asks if they have caught any fish—and they probably shouted back, "We have Peter," which meant they did not catch anything all night. Jesus tells them to cast their nets to the right side of the boat, and there they caught so many fish that once again their nets were breaking.

Now John, who was a contemplative and lay on the breast of Jesus at the Last Supper, nudged Peter and said, "Peter, this is Jesus." Peter, the impulsive one, put on his cloak, jumped into the water, and ran to meet Jesus while John stayed on the boat.

And so Peter does not change, neither does John the contemplative or Thomas the doubter. Mary Magdalene, the crazy lover before the Resurrection, is equally crazy afterward when she is in the cemetery looking for the dead body of Jesus. What would she have done if she found it? But Jesus approached her, lovingly calling her by name. She recognized the sound of his voice and her heart responded. She knew this was Jesus, and she became the first witness and apostle of the Resurrection. So Mary Magdalene does not change. And we have seen earlier that Paul had to deal with his "thorn in the flesh" till he died. He too does not change.

If all the stalwarts in the Gospels do not change, why are you and I struggling to overcome our weaknesses and attachments by our own willpower, though we barely make any progress? But *something* changed in all these people. The love and the life of God are shining bright and clear in the hearts and the lives of all of them. Their individual weaknesses, still present, now make them so charming and their lives so enchanting and attractive. These dark areas give them a special flavor, and God works through them. The negative becomes a positive through the transformative energy of God's grace.

How do we change then? What can we do?

I remember many, many years ago when I first began to give directed retreats, there was a nun who came to me weeping uncontrollably. She had been working on a weakness of hers for many years. It was like a huge rock in her life and after all these years of struggling to overcome it, all she managed to do was to chip off a little bit on the top. She was disappointed, frustrated, and had reached the state of desperation.

In my innocence I suggested that rather than getting rid of the rock, she could make a rock garden. Grow some nice little plants and flowers. And thanks to your rock this garden will have an attractive character.

The plants and flowers would stand for all that was beautiful in her life—her talents and her gifts and all the good that she did, bringing joy, happiness, and meaning into the lives of so many in ways small and great. Her garden would stand for the people who came into her life, making her feel worthwhile and happy.

Now if she focused only on the rock with all her will-power, she would keep chipping off just little bits, and at the end of the day and at the end of her life she would feel frustrated and hopeless because the garden would have dis-appeared. She would have focused all her energy on some rock and would have lived a wasted life. But if she spent that same energy on the garden, with its plants and flowers, at the end of her life she would feel so content and happy. And thanks to her rock, she and her garden of life would be so very unique and attractive.

There's a story about a man on a long business trip who came upon an out-of-the-way shop in a city he was visiting in France one evening. He found a rock that intrigued him. It looked like an ordinary rock, but the shopkeeper showed him how each of the cracks in the rock would shine with different colored lights in the dark. The businessman bought it for his wife as a symbol of their love and as a sign that he carried her with him wherever he traveled. He packed the rock carefully in his suitcase.

About a month later, he returned home and, very excited, asked his wife to turn off the lights. He took out the rock but nothing happened. He began to yell, "I've been cheated. I paid a lot of money for this!" His wife turned the lights on and asked her husband to explain what he meant. He told her that he had picked up the expensive rock as a symbol of his love for her. Then he explained that each of the rock's cracks was supposed to glow with a different colored light in the dark. She graciously accepted the rock, put it back in its box, and kissed him lovingly.

The next day the wife took the box to her neighbor next door to ask what was written on the outside in French. It is a simple instruction, the neighbor said: "If you want me to shine in the dark, expose me to the sunlight." Because the man had kept the rock wrapped up and sitting in his suitcase for about a month it couldn't shine. So after placing the rock in the sunlight, the wife surprised her husband that night. Every one of the cracks in the rock gave off a different color, making the whole rock look enchanting and beautiful.

Life has broken us all in many different ways. Physically we cannot do the same things we did so easily a few years ago. Emotionally we have been hurt by people we work with, those we live with, and those whom we love deeply. Fear, guilt, and anxiety sometimes break us spiritually. Every one of these cracks in our lives glows with a radiance that makes us attractive and beautiful people. As St. Paul writes, "Where sin increased, grace overflowed all the more." This does not mean that we should go on sinning or breaking ourselves even more. Life will do that to us. But then it is life's opportunity to show off its brilliance. We become attractive people radiating through our weakness the Divine presence and breath that reside within us.

Many years ago I was told of some priests in a certain country who had drinking problems and of their bishop, who had abandoned them to the remote parts of the diocese. The amazing thing was that during Lent, when Catholics went to confession, they would travel miles to search out these priests. The people were sure that these weak men would understand. These holy men would be more compassionate than the ones who were kept in high places. Just as St. Paul writes that God's power is manifested in his weakness, in our weakness we find the strength of the compassion of God.

And then I remember my friends I met in Taizé, France. I shared a room with John Daries, who was there with his friend Wilma Jacobsen. Wilma was an Anglican deaconess at the time and wanted me to journey with her as she made her discernment to be ordained a priest.

John and Wilma were from South Africa and were actively involved in the liberation of that country. Wilma worked with Winnie Mandela, and John was often on the run from the police because of his involvement in organizing the people to win their freedom. John and Wilma shared with me this story that they used to empower people:

> One time Archbishop Tutu and then-president Botha were traveling in a little boat. A strong wind blew and the hat that the president was wearing flew off his head and was floating on the water. Archbishop Tutu, being an archbishop, got out of the boat, walked on the water, and brought the president's hat back to him. The next day the newspaper headlines screamed: ARCHBISHOP TUTU CANNOT SWIM!

John and Wilma used this story to make the oppressed South Africans aware of how much people were telling them about things they could not do. No one was telling them about the many great things that they were already doing and the even greater things that they were capable of doing. No one was telling them about the greatness of their ancestors.

With my family, my friends, the people I work with, those I worship with, if I can just focus on the wonderful things that they are doing, have done, and are capable of doing, sooner or later, I believe, we will all be walking on water.

And so we have a choice. It all depends on where you are putting your focus, where you are putting your energy. If you direct your energy on overcoming your sin and disordered affections, they will grow, they will get more disordered. But if your focus is on deepening your relationship with God, that relationship will grow and it will take care of your disordered affections and all the rest.

12

Pain Is a Fact of Life, Misery Is a State of Mind

One of the great illusions of humankind is that we're supposed to suffer. We don't have to suffer.

Suffering is too often confused with pain. Pain is a fact of life. It's there—we can't escape it. Suffering, on the other hand, is a state of mind. The Buddhists believe that life is full of suffering caused by craving for and attachment to the transitory and changing things in life. But there is a way out of suffering, and that is to attain a state of equanimity, or learning to find a balance in life. We do not need to cling to the good things in life, the good feelings and positive experiences. Neither do we need to struggle to get rid of the painful parts of our life. We need to learn to live through the pains and joys of our lives in order to live a full and happy life—one without suffering.

Pain in life has a purpose. It can be a good thing. Pain, when not resisted, always purifies and enlightens. Pain that is resisted becomes suffering. This is true in many parts of our lives, including and especially in our relationships with others and with the Divine. Pain enlightens us about who we are, who God is, and what life is all about.

The cross of Jesus is not a glorification of suffering, but it is the Good News in action. The Good News is liberation, not *from* suffering, sickness, and death, but freedom *in* suffering, sickness, and even in death. The cross of Jesus is the consequence of his life and teaching. The cross reminds us that life does not owe us pleasure but offers us meaning.

So suffering is pain that is resisted. When I resist pain, then I suffer. Pain is a fact of life; misery is a state of mind.

So in other words, we can do without suffering. The great and famous French artist Auguste Renoir developed severe arthritis later in his life and found it painful even to hold a brush. It tortured his friends to see Renoir in so much pain, and they asked him to stop painting. But Renoir—who toward the end would strap a brush to his paralyzed fingers in order to keep painting—exclaimed, "Pain passes but beauty remains forever."

Consider something from our daily lives, something as simple as walking: for some elderly or injured people, when they walk they have pain. But they want to walk. So they do and feel the pain. They cannot do away with the pain, but they know that there is more to life than the hurt they experience. Or for those of us who are younger and more healthy, walking can still sometimes be painful, like when our feet hurt. But if we resist the pain, we will go nowhere. Walking with the pain on the other hand takes us to places we would not have gone otherwise. So this is when we are opening ourselves to experience God in all things.

Now I am not glorifying pain—if you have a headache, go take an aspirin. But suppose the pain we're talking about is the pain of loss, like the loss of a parent or a close friend. That is painful. But if I keep thinking, *Why did this happen? It should not have happened. Why is God so unfair as to allow this?* then I am going to suffer. But if I can deal with the pain of my father's death or my mother's death or my friend's death, that somehow purifies me and gives me a better understanding of reality, a better understanding of myself, and opens me to a greater, freer experience of the Divine and of life.

The Buddhists have a unique way of dealing with pain in life. When something painful happens, they do not spend too much time wondering *why* this happened to them. They do spend their time thinking, "Now that this has happened to me, *how* do I want to live the rest of my life?" If a Buddhist loses an arm in an accident, he or she does not sit and cry all their life wondering why this had to happen to them. The Buddhist would rather explore all the infinite possibilities of living effectively and fully with one arm.

This is an effective way of living through pain in any situation in our lives. Suppose the doctor tells me that I have a short time to live. If I really think about how I want to live the time that is given to me, I will probably live my life more fully than all the years when I thought I had many still ahead. There is a very telling story of a man who came down with a fatal illness. The doctors told him that he had a rare illness and would not live for more than three years.

The man sat down to think about this and decided to reassess his life and way of living. There was so little that would upset him now. He always reminded himself that he had just three years to live, and so he did not find it worthwhile worrying about all the securities that people are so anxious about; he was not affected by the negative behavior of people toward him; the material things that he had valued so much and had been attached to he was now able to let go of; he gave these possessions away so others would enjoy them. Because after all, he had just three years to live.

He looked around and noticed so many marvels of God's creation that he had ignored and now began to enjoy; he thought of all those who were near and dear to him whom he had taken for granted and he reached out to them—the letter he had wanted to write and had been putting off for another day, the lonely relative he had wanted to call or visit, the lost friendship he had wanted to renew—he did it. All that he wanted to do he now began to do. Because he had just three years to live.

Then one day the man's doctors called him to the office all excited. They were overjoyed to tell him that a cure was found for his illness. When the man heard this, he broke down and cried! He was afraid that he would revert to his previous way of living. When he thought he had just three years to live, he had begun to live life to the fullest—one day at a time and as completely as he could.

Then there is the story of a man who called his wife from the doctor's office. He was crying bitterly as he told his wife that he had bad news. And his wife, very concerned, asked him what was wrong. He told her that the doctor had asked him to take a pill a day for the rest of his life. And his wife gave a sigh of relief and responded, "Honey, that's not so bad. I know many, many people who take a pill—and some who take more than a pill—every day for the rest of their lives, and they live happily for a very long time." "I know," said her husband, "but the doctor has given me only four pills."

Now maybe the doctor has given you forty pills or four hundred pills. We have but a short time here to live. So the question before us is, how do we really want to live? As the saying goes, if you had just fifteen minutes to live and one phone call to make, who would you call, what would you say—and why are you waiting?

Think about other times and situations in our lives we could apply this approach. How about when I lose a parent at the time when I need them most, or a spouse to death or unfaithfulness, or a child to some addiction? What about times when I have made mistakes and experience failure? Yes, it is important to find out the reasons for all of this, but it is certainly more helpful and healthy to find ways of making the rest of our lives more meaningful and fulfilling.

So it is through both joy and pain that we are guided to clarity and faith in our relationship with God. We don't have to wait for the good times and pleasurable situations to experience God. With this way of living we have yet another means of opening ourselves to a continuing and ever-greater experience of life and of the Divine.

13

Reinforcing a Divine Experience to Nurture It

God's seduction of each of us, as powerful an experience as it is, is just the beginning of our romance with the Divine. The experience draws us in and changes us. But the newfound knowledge of ourselves and of our relationship with God needs to be nurtured.

God seduced me at a young age, drawing me into a greater awareness of my authentic self. And as I've said, every time a person's relationship with God deepens, he or she has a greater sense of their own sinfulness. So as God's seduction drew me in, I began to look deep into my own sin. I discovered that my root sin, my personal shadow, was the fear of being alone and the fear of abandonment. This is at the root of my sinfulness, and it manifests itself in so many ways. I have been at times hypercritical of people and unconsciously tried to destroy their God-given gifts through my rash judgment and sharp criticism. I had wanted to bring them into my area of loneliness. I tried to win the love of people by compromising myself. I sacrificed all I had—my very self—just to get some love from someone. I spent years of my life feeling miserable about myself. These were times of great loneliness and quiet desperation.

Two experiences from my youth are insightful. The first was a story told by a Jesuit priest who went around preaching retreats to schoolkids. This particular story made a deep impression on me: A village once put on a play and the participants in the play were from all walks of life. There was a teacher and a student, a parent, a priest and a nun, a cab driver and a bus driver, a doctor and a politician—all walks of life were represented in that play. At the end of the play a judge came to award the prize for the best actor. "And the prize for the best actor goes to," the judge began, and paused to create an anticipation in the people. "The prize for the best actor goes to . . . the beggar!" Now everyone in the village applauded except the man who played the king. This man said, "I acted as the king. I should be given the prize for the best actor." And he was told categorically that he was just a poor insignificant man in the village acting as a king. But the beggar was actually a rich and famous man, and so he deserved the prize for the best actor. And then this Jesuit who told the story, along with another who would go around to schools giving Act of Contrition retreats, gave a long and convincing talk on humility. Of course, their definition of humility was being worthless and good for nothing.

These Jesuit missionaries who seemed to come right out of the Spanish Inquisition succeeded in instilling fear and guilt not only in me but in my parents and the Catholic community in India. We did not think that true humility was acknowledging the gifts and talents we received from God. Instead, we thought that true humility was stripping our-selves like the rich man did when he played the beggar. We took that beggar home and made ourselves into his image and likeness. We wanted to be sure that on the last day when the Eternal King comes to give out the prizes for the best actors, we would qualify.

I developed a deep inferiority complex and a very poor self-image. Even though I knew that I was gifted, I was never happy. I felt so lonely that I remember praying with tears in my eyes a prayer that came from the depths of my being: "Lord, take away all my talents, but give me one person who would love me for myself." And God answered my prayer. But instead of taking away all of my talents and gifts, God set me on a path to discover my true identity so that I could use my talents more freely and effectively, and live a happier life.

I was in my midtwenties and was watching the Olympics on television. It was the 100-meter race, and I was at the starting line with the other runners. "On your marks . . . set . . . ," and then I was off with the bang, running with the one who stood first. The world's fastest runner! I identified myself with him as my hair stood on end. I watched soccer and the same thing happened to me when someone would score a goal and run to his fans. My hair stood on end as if I had scored that goal.

I decided to take this experience to my spiritual director and that was a turning point in my life. My spiritual direc-tor had known me since I was twelve. When I shared this experience of the Olympics with him, he told me that he would never forget a day in my life when I was in high school. It was Sports Day, and I was leaving the school grounds as the overall Champion of the Day. I was carrying the championship trophy, my father and mother were carrying some of my other trophies, and so were my sisters and brother.

My spiritual director came up to my father and said, "Congratulations, Mr. Coutinho! You must be proud of your son today." And my father heard the word *"proud"* and responded spontaneously, "He did not win the cycling prize!" My poor father did not want any of us to go to hell. Remember, the beggar in the previous story was our model to win the Eternal Prize on the Last Day.

So I was Champion of the Day, had won all the races except the cycling race. In most of the races I had placed first; I placed a few seconds, but no thirds. And yet our focus—the cycling race. I remember that we were poor then, and in our small home my mother put a sheet over a table to display all the trophies. And we sat around and guess what we talked about? The cycling race! I had the most ordinary bicycle because we could not rent a more sophisticated one, and a little before the race one of the other kids let some air out of my tires. With those disadvantages I raced. I was not the last one to finish, but I was not among the top three.

I carried the cycling-prize syndrome for years. But my experience of that Olympics in my twenties made me a real champion once again. A real champion! I looked back on my life and I realized that in my relationship with God, I was a champion. I had committed only one mortal sin: I once had said, "Bloody" and then had run to confession, sure I would go to hell for that. And yet with all the good that I had done and was doing, I was so uncomfortable in my relationship with God. When I reflected on my relationships with people, I realized that I could not keep a friendship simply because I would always remain focused on something in the friendship that I should not have said or done, however insignificant that might have been. My friends would try to bring my attention to all the wonderful and positive things in the friendship, but I would insist on "the cycling prize" in the relationship. I did the same in my work and ministry. I was gifted and God had blessed me with many talents. I did a lot of good, but of course I looked for something to go wrong or something that was negative. And every time I experienced rejection in a relationship, or was criticized for something I had done, or fell short in my religious practice, it would hurt me deeply. But then I would turn to my image of the beggar and draw consolation that this image was being perfected in me and my chances for the Eternal Reward were a little more certain.

I went to a close friend of mine at this time and talked to him. I shared with him my experience of the Olympics and said, "You know my problem, I know my problem. I suffer from a deep inferiority complex and have a very negative self-image. Can you help me?" And he said, "Sure." And then he gave me my mantra: "I'm important, I'm precious, and I have something beautiful to offer—that's me!" I took this mantra and began to repeat it a hundred, a thousand times every day: "I am important, precious, and beautiful!"

But I needed something to hold onto to reinforce my mantra. When we are insecure, because we feel negative about ourselves, we need something to hold onto that reinforces our experiences of our true selves and of the Divine, lest we lose them. So after getting my mantra, I used everything to nurture it. I used the Bible, I used my life experience, I used my memory and imagination. When I turned to the Bible, I found so many Scripture passages that supported my mantra. The first two chapters of Genesis reminded me that I am created in God's image and likeness. In fact, I am the Divine breath. God did not make junk when I was created. I prayed Isaiah 43:4, 7, "You are precious in my eyes and I love you. . . . I have created you for my glory," and this began to slowly but surely sink in. And Isaiah 49:14–16 says: "I will never forget you. See, upon the palms of my hands I have written your name." Luke 12:22–32 convinced me that I am worth more than the birds of the air and the lilies of the field. And so many other passages in the Bible kept reinforcing my mantra: important, precious, and beautiful! I realized that even if I do not know it or feel it, I will always be important, precious and beautiful—because God has created me that way.

Then I also reflected back over my life and began to see my whole life again in a different way, a positive way. As I said, in the past all that I did was look for where I had not measured up; if ten people, or even a hundred people, said good things about me, I would latch onto that one negative thing that one person said about me, however true or false. Now I went back over my life, and there—in those same relationships—I found all these positive things. I found those hundreds of people I had overlooked who were saying good things about me and experiencing good things in their relationship with me and doing good things that reinforced my mantra. I came out of this nurturing experience with a new vision of who I was and of who God was. So everything in my life up to that moment was the same, and yet everything had changed.

I took my mantra and this new vision of myself into my relationship with God and with people. I took my mantra into my ministry. Soon I didn't need to rely on the Bible and past memories to tell me who I was because I began to experience it in my daily life. My relationship with God grew by leaps and bounds and so did my relationships with people. I was able to get into daring and very challenging ministry and be very effective. Because now I knew, I do not have to win the cycling prize to be important, precious, and beautiful. Now I simply feel it at the core of my being.

I have shared this mantra and ways of reinforcing it with people in India and different parts of the world, and today so many people are using this effectively. It does not have a copyright—it's not mine. You are welcome to try it or find your own. I encourage you to.

Whether this mantra suits you or not, the point of my story is this: once I was able to look through my root sin and find my true self, then yielding to and accepting God's seductive love was easy. It was natural. It flowed.

2

Romancing God

14

The Desert Experience

What happens when we fall into God's seduction? We begin a Divine romance. This romance always blooms first in the barrenness of the desert. Let me explain . . .

If you want to fall in love with God, it's not going to be all rainbows and butterflies—there's a price to pay. When you allow yourself to be seduced by God, God will lead you into the desert.

Each of us has a desert experience waiting inside us—a barren place or cave deep within us where the Divine dwells and where we find our true selves. The desert is a place of letting go; you let go of all your securities because in the desert there is nothing that you can hold onto. Whether you take the desert as a symbol or literally—in the desert there are no structures, there are no road maps. There's no family, no social constructs, no culture, no religion. So the desert is a scary place, but it's also one of cleansing and transcending. In the desert you experience God in nakedness, and you experience yourself in nakedness—without any masks, without any defenses. You see yourself as you really are, and you see God as God is. And you begin to experience all of life as it truly is.

Jesus had a desert experience. At his baptism in the Jordan River, God seduced Jesus with a profound and mystical relationship with the Divine: "You are my beloved Son; with you I am well pleased." And once Jesus has this awesome intimate encounter, he was immediately taken—"the Spirit drove him" the Bible says—into the desert. There he faced and transcended the core human temptations: the temptation to find the meaning of life and the source of happiness in the material things of this world, to find these in human honor and glory, and to find these in power and authority. In the desert Jesus overcame these temptations in order to find his meaning and happiness solely in the Divine and to assume his true identity and mission. The Divine romance that began at his baptism would continue through the Transfiguration, which prepared Jesus for his passion and death, and would climax in the Resurrection.

Similarly, once St. Paul had his experience of the Divine seduction on the way to Damascus, he too was taken into the desert. Paul had this tremendous experience of God, lost his sight, and then could not eat or regain any strength for three days. Paul was drawn into the desert where he says: "I did not immediately consult flesh and blood, nor did I go up to Jerusalem to those who were apostles before me" (Galatians 1:16–17). He was on his own in the desert. It was in the desert where Paul had to let go of his security in the Mosaic law and find the freedom that comes from Jesus' Good News that God loves him totally and unconditionally. Paul's romance with

the Divine would take him through the depths of weakness
and suffering and bring him through the heights of mystical experience. He was shown what "no eye has seen" and
heard what "no ear has heard." Paul was given an out-of-body
experience—he experienced his real self as he truly was in
the Divine.

And then there's St. Ignatius, who was seduced on his
sickbed by the chivalry of the saints in their relationship
with the Divine. Later, he was drawn into a cave, literally,
in Manresa. He spent a year there—meditating, praying,
reflecting on his life, and begging for food. He was slowly
stripped of everything, every idea about himself that he had
previously clung to, until in his nakedness and surrender he
was brought to grace. His time in the desert ended with a
profound experience of God by the banks of Cardoner River,
where he recognized God as "schoolmaster" in his life. God
as schoolmaster gave him insight into Divine mysteries and
the mysteries of everyday life. This experience became for
Ignatius the absolute guiding principle—for the rest of his
life—in dealing with persons, institutions, and life itself.

Ignatius's romance with the Divine forced him to let go
of control over his life. Once he allowed God to lead him, he
was given insight into the mysteries of the Divine. In a little
chapel at La Storta just outside Rome, Ignatius had a mystical
experience in which he sees himself being placed with Jesus,
and God the Father instructs Jesus to take Ignatius as his
companion. In this experience Ignatius put on the mind and
consciousness of Christ—in which for God there is "neither
Jew nor Greek, there is neither slave nor free person, there

is not male and female" (Galatians 3:28). Now, like Paul, as
a child of God, Ignatius is a Divine heir. The romance continued and so did the revelations. In another mystical experience, Jesus then placed Ignatius *in* the Trinity—Ignatius saw
himself within the Trinity. The Divine dance of Ignatius ends
with his decisive mystical experience: he finds himself lost in
the very being and essence of the Divine. And Ignatius would
have never experienced any of this had he not been willing to
be led by God into the cave at Manresa.

The desert experience is not limited to Christians. The
Buddha was seduced by the Divine through four basic experiences of life: old age, sickness, death, and the freedom of the
wandering mendicant. His Divine romance took him first to
the great teachers whose teaching he mastered but brought
him neither peace nor freedom. The same thing happened
when he followed the rigors of asceticism. It almost killed him
but did not give him what his heart was seeking. He finally sat
in meditation under a tree for forty-nine days and found his
enlightenment that he expressed as the Middle Way.

The Prophet Mohammed was also lured by God
through his disgust with the desecration of the sacred altar
that Abraham had set up. This was the seduction that brought
him into a romance with the Divine in a cave during the
month of Ramadan, when he was fasting. The angel Gabriel
revealed to him God's word that is engraved in heaven and
drew him into a reverent and intimate relationship with the
Divine.

Jesus, Paul, Ignatius, the Buddha, and the Prophet
Mohammed—they all came back from their deserts with a
totally new vision of the love of the Divine, of themselves,

and of life. Their Divine romance drove them to teach and invite others to the Divine dance.

And here's the important point: you don't stay in the desert. After being changed in the desert you come out, you come back to the world. There you find that nothing has changed, but everything has changed.

15

Are You Finding God in Life—or Are You Encountering God in Your Life?

In your own Divine romance you will encounter God again and again and again. Each time, God will come on God's own terms, and the romance deepens. But this happens only when you are willing to encounter God as God is.

"Finding God in all things" is a motto used by many to express their spiritual way of life. This phrase seems to me a very Western orientation. It indicates that it is by your own effort that you will find God. But in the East we view things differently; we allow God to find us, and then there is no telling when this God will appear and in what form. This is an important distinction in one's deepening romance with the Divine.

When we are "finding God in all things," the initiative is ours and so we will find the God that we are looking for. When we are sick, we will look for a God who knows something about medicine. And when we are cured, we will give this God great thanks and forget about this God until the next illness. Now when we are preparing for an important exam, we expect a God who is smart to respond to our prayer. Once again when we get good results, we give this God thanks and seek this God out at the next exam. To help us with our financial problems we need a God who is a good banker. We may even give part of our wealth and earnings to some charity after this banker God helps us.

But when we allow God to find us, then we do not know the time or the manner in which we will encounter God. We have a funny story in India. The Hindu religion believes in the celebration of life. Their 330 million gods—all expressions of experiences of *one* God—are celebrated each year when images of the gods are installed in the temple, in the homes, and in neighborhoods, worshipped with daily rituals for a short period of time, and then ceremoniously thrown into the sea amidst great dancing, music, and joy. So the story goes that a Hindu man was once drowning and called out for help to all the gods he could think of. For a long time there was no answer. Then one of the gods appeared to him. But when he appeared, instead of helping the drowning man, this god began to dance with glee. The man was confused and begged the god to help, but the only answer the drowning man got was "Every year when I am drowned in the waters, you dance. So why are you complaining?"

When God finds us, rather than coming down to help us or carry us or do for us the very specific things we ask, we hear a voice that says "Do you really want to get well? Then *you* take up your mat and walk. Do you really want to see? Then *you* open your eyes and see." God has *already* given us the strength, everything we need, all that is necessary for this life; we have the power, we have the gifts, we have the talents and blessings—it's at our disposal as children of God, heirs of the Divine. All we need to access the Divine grace is the faith to claim it as our right.

All through the Gospels, Jesus wants people to have faith and believe. Instead of faith he either gets fear or awe. These are people who are finding God. The classical example of this is when Jesus is out at sea with his inner circle, the apostles, the foundation of his church, and he asks them to launch out into the deep and then falls asleep. They are caught in a storm and the apostles are terrified. They wake up Jesus, complaining, "Lord, save us! We are perishing!" And Jesus says, "Why are you terrified, O you of little faith?" and calms the winds and the sea. Now, you would think that this would have *helped* the faith and belief of his future church. Instead they are now in awe and amazement—but no belief! The remarkable thing is that this passage is in all three synoptic Gospels and is placed in the midst of the many miracles that are being worked by Jesus because of the faith of simple people. It is often the pagans, such as Samaritans, who have the faith, and Jesus commends them. These religious and social outcasts have nowhere to turn and nothing to hold onto, and so when God finds them they discover their inner strength and extraordinary capability. Their faith can move mountains.

When we find God, our capacity is limited and so are our possibilities. But if we allow God to take the lead then there are infinite possibilities beyond our current imagination. Look at the story of the boy who was greedy for sweets. His mother takes him to the bishop who offers him sweets in a box, and the boy refuses to take any until the bishop finally gives him a handful. On their way home the mother questions the greedy boy: Why didn't he take the sweets that the bishop was offering? The boy had a smirk on his face and said, "My hand is small but the bishop's hand is big." God is more generous than any bishop.

We need to look at our attitude in our romance with God—are we encountering or finding God in all things? When we find God, we are in control, but when we *encounter* God, there is no telling what will happen to us. We are not in control. God finds us and God's love is in control. We can only fall back on faith and the inner strength that flows from our true identity. But these latter two—unlike our illusions of control—are real, true, and lasting without change. So in your relationship with God, seek not to find, but to encounter God.

Here's another beautiful and unexpected example of how God finds us. Sometime last year, I was giving a retreat to a Jesuit in Goa, India. Now the Jesuits in Goa have a beautiful retreat house on the beach. And of course on a beachfront you have all the lights and the glitter and the entertainment and everything that's there—and it looks more like a carnival. But this Jesuit told me that he has always been fascinated by darkness. He loves darkness. He said he thought this whole idea of the infinite and of trying to go beyond the infinite in the spiritual life was just a cute idea until he began to look into and contemplate darkness. In his contemplative prayer he was gripped by darkness, and he went to penetrate that darkness, and he went to see the darkness and its greater and greater darkness, until he all of a sudden broke down and began to cry. Because in that infinite darkness, he encountered the infinite energy; he encountered a God that had gone beyond anything he knew of God, anything he ever expected from God, anything he ever thought possible of God. Through darkness. The darkness enveloped him and God overtook him. This is letting God find you.

16

Prayer: The Language of Divine Romance

In our romance with God there is a language through which this loving relationship is communicated, deepens, and grows. That language is prayer. We can't discuss our Divine romance without discussing prayer—what it is, its forms and stages, and some techniques and tools I or others have used that may be of help to you.

What Happens When God Finds You

Prayer is the most common way we relate to and grow in our relationship with God. But what is prayer? It is an experience that happens when God finds us. When I go to pray, I do not go to find God, but when I pray, I allow God to find me. Again, this is not just a play on words; the two approaches are very different, and choosing the latter will have a great effect in deepening and expanding our relationship with God.

With the perspective of encountering God, I begin my prayer by becoming aware of God waiting to affect my life.

God is waiting to take over my life. St. Paul tells us that we do not know how to pray as we ought, but if we let the Spirit pray within us, God hears that prayer (Romans 8:26).

I remember attending a recital of the *Bhagavad Gita* where Swami Chinmayananda was the guest of honor. After the recital was finished and Swamiji got up to talk, he shared a story to describe the person who had recited the sacred verses: There was a rich man whose interior decorator advised him that he would need a picture four feet by six for his bedroom. So the man came to the city where he was taken by a friend to meet an artist. This person was a real artist. The artist showed the rich man all kinds of paintings and then suggested a particularly outstanding one. The rich man asked if it measured four feet by six and then went on to ask two questions that you do not ask a true artist: first, how much did it cost? The artist casually replied something like one thousand dollars. The rich man thought for a while and then asked the second—could he have four copies, please?

Swamiji went on to say that a piece of art cannot be repeated because an artist starts to paint but soon the artist is so lost in the painting that the painting begins to come out of the artist. The art is a once-in-a-lifetime experience and cannot be duplicated. It had been the same with the recital that evening, Swamiji said. The woman who was singing the sacred songs began singing but soon the song came out of her.

We do not know how to grow in our prayer life, as Paul says, but if we pray with the attitude that God is waiting to affect our lives, soon the Spirit begins to pray from deep within us. With no words but simple presence, the Spirit flows within us and the prayer comes out of us. Just as it is difficult to tell a good dancer from the dance or a good actor from the character they are portraying, here the prayer and the pray-er become one. The Spirit flows within the person and, over time, that Divine prayer experience will flow into everything he or she does, and then all of life is prayer.

Deepening the Divine Romance

"The world is charged with the grandeur of God" wrote the poet Gerard Manley Hopkins. The French Jesuit and mystic Teilhard de Chardin believed that we live in the divine milieu. And St. Ignatius experienced a powerful revelation on the banks of the River Cardoner in which he saw all of creation manifesting the Divine love and God laboring through all creation for our benefit and our own spiritual and divine transformation. All life, then, is an experience of the Divine. So if we go to pray and do not experience God and deepen our relationship with the Divine, then maybe our prayer was just a formality or an empty ritual.

Prayer is a *means*, not an end in itself. Prayer is a means to deepen my relationship with the Divine. I pray to expand my experience of God and through my prayer my God gets bigger and bigger and bigger. We could say the same thing about every aspect of our lives—our work and ministry, schooling and parenting, health and sickness, good times and bad times—all of it is a manifestation of our Divine romance.

Thomas Aquinas tells us that God is always bigger than what we can ever think about God. Augustine will tell us that anyone who says that he or she has understood God knows nothing about God. Now we do not need Aquinas or Augustine to tell us these things. Common sense will tell us that God is always bigger than anything we can know of God and deeper than any experience we can have of the Divine. So God is always bigger than whatever we think about or the way we relate to God at any given moment. Prayer is a means to expand our concept and our experience to make our God bigger and greater. That's the purpose of prayer, and that is the purpose of life itself—the realization of the Divine or finding our identity in the Divine.

One technique for growing in our relationship with God is to reflect on our prayer experience. This is often called a review of prayer. People, after finishing their prayer, will reflect on how well they did in the contemplation or meditation. If they did poorly, they will look for reasons and perhaps express sorrow in order to do better in the future. If they did well, they will thank God and try to do more of the same the next time. Now let's look into this. Let's look at this question, "How well did I do?" "Did I succeed in my prayer?"

When we reflect on how well we did, the center of attention is definitely on ourselves. Our focus is on our distractions in prayer and the resolutions we make at the end of the prayer. And we realize after years of this exercise that neither the distractions nor the resolutions seem to change. In fact, when I was first taught to make my review of prayer and asked to reflect on how well I did, my review soon filtered into a short statement: "Prayer? Good. Distractions. Improving." Now you were not sure if the prayer was improving or the distractions were. I was finding God in my prayer and not letting God find me.

A little humorous but the point is, when we review our prayer time or when we talk about our prayer to a friend, a priest, our spiritual director, whomever—how many of us talk about our distractions? How many of us focus on, *How do I overcome my distractions?* But this is not having a relationship with God; this is having a relationship with our distractions. This is not falling in love with God or romancing God; this is a one-way street of us having a relationship with ourselves. What we really want to talk about, what we really want to look at is Where was God in all of this? How was God affecting us? How was God moving us? How was God drawing us into a deeper relationship with the Divine?

So prayer is not about finding God, prayer is about allowing God to find us—in whatever way and form God is working in our lives. If my review of prayer is focused on what God was doing in my prayer, then every review would be different, a romance and an adventure. Now that's an important difference. In other words: what happened to me? *What happened to me?* is where I encounter the Divine. *What happened to me?* is not like asking how well I did. This question flips everything around. Now it's not what *I* was doing in my prayer that I reflect on but what *God* was doing in my prayer. How was God affecting me in my prayer? I don't judge but instead seek to perceive how—through the positive or negative—God is drawing me deeper into Divine intimacy to experience my own spiritual and divine identity.

Similarly, when I minister to people through my speaking or retreats, or when I am with you here on the written page, it is not me communicating God to you. I make myself available to God so that God will be able to work in me and through me to affect others. That is the encounter. I am not in control of what will happen to you. If you think I am sharing

this book to change you—well, that's what I used to think
before I fell in love with God. When I was younger, I wanted
to impress everybody with my knowledge and spirituality; I
wanted everybody to follow my way to God. *By the time you
finish hearing what I have to say, you have to be changed and be
different!* Of course I wanted to make sure everyone changed,
to experience and become a part of the kingdom of God. No.
This is God's work. I do not take on God's responsibility.
What I do on my part is let myself go, in God, and let God
work in me and through me. I am confident in the God that
I believe in. I am confident that in my encounter with God,
the Divine is at work in me. And I do not control or seek to
control *your* encounter with God, which may or may not be
happening as you read my words or hear me speak. That is
your romance with Divine.

So when you pray or when you reflect on your day, try
asking these questions: "Where was God? What was God
doing? What was God leading me away from or toward?"
The focus is on God, on your beloved. And when you pray
like this, when you examine God's presence and not yourself, you will find that every experience will be different. It
has to be different, because God will always draw you deeper
into this romantic relationship. God will always take you to
a different place.

17

Three Paradigms of Prayer

I would like to use three paradigms of prayer that can help us in our romance with the Divine.

The First Paradigm: From Talking to Silence

The first paradigm has four stages. Most of us begin our prayer life and our relationship with God by talking to God and believing that God listens to us. At this first stage we feel that we can bring all our needs to God, trusting that what our loved ones cannot do or provide for us, God will certainly be able to. Then as we grow in our spiritual life, we are told that we need to listen to God because God wants to speak to us. And so like the boy Samuel in the Bible, we too say, "Speak, Lord, for your servant is listening." We listen for what God wants us to do. We look for God's will for us. We want to be pleasing to God, and we begin to look into ourselves and see what God wants us to change. We work on our weaknesses and our sinfulness. So in the first stage we talk, God listens; in the second stage, God talks, we listen. Then, as our relationship with God grows ever deeper, we encounter the third stage: we listen to God while God is also listening. Prayer now is without words, without requests from either side. It is a prayer of the heart. God is now not an idea or a symbol, but a prevailing presence. So we listen and God listens. The final stage of prayer is when no one talks and no one listens. There is silence. This prayer of silence is the surest and most direct way to union with the Divine. There are very few obstacles, if any, between you and the Divine. Silence is like Mary being overshadowed by the Holy Spirit, Moses drawn into a cloud and transformed, Jesus transfigured on Mount Tabor.

The Second Paradigm: Stages of a Love Relationship

The second paradigm is one given to us by a great Indian mystic, Adi Shankaracharya. Prayer, we are told, is a means of deepening our relationship with the Divine, and just as our human relationships go through four stages, so does our relationship with the Divine. We begin our human relationships with words. When we first meet someone and begin to fall in love, we spend a lot of time talking. We want to share with this newfound love as much as possible about ourselves. And so we keep talking about our life, our likes and dislikes, and how our day was. We talk about our parents, our brothers and sisters, our aunts and uncles, our past experiences, our present reality, and our future dreams; we talk endlessly about our successes and failures. Through all these words we want to communicate to the other person "You mean a lot to me and I love you."

Our relationship with God begins in the same way. I remember when I was little my mother put me on her lap and the first prayer she taught me was, "Jesus, please bless me. Make me a big boy and a good boy. Bless my daddy and give him lots of money. Bless my mummy and give her good health." So I had begun my relationship with God and would pray and ask God to take me safely to school and bring me safely back. I asked for help in my exams and prayed for all my friends. I soon learned prayers of praise and thanksgiving. All vocal prayers were a part of the first stage in my relationship with God.

Now when a relationship grows deeper, words become inadequate to express this deeper love. In fact, words are sometimes what St. Paul calls resounding gongs and noisy cymbals. Words can be easily misunderstood, and they can seldom express feelings or capture an experience. We come now to the "show me" stage. Here we look to signs and symbols to express our love for our beloved. A card, a gift, flowers, a handshake, a hug, a meaningful look, a kiss, or an embrace are all sacred signs to express a love that is now deeper than words. We now want *to do* something for our beloved to express our love. We might cook a special meal, arrange a favorite outing, or alleviate some burdensome task for this person. These things we do are signs and symbols of our deep love. The same thing happens to us in our relationship with God. When our love for God grows, we want to do something to show God that we love God more than words. Then the words of Scripture that say "Whatever you do to the least of my brothers and sisters you do to me" becomes our way of life. We go out of our way to reach out to those in need and offer ourselves—sometimes even sacrifice ourselves—for others. We believe that when we are serving our neighbor, we are serving God.

A word of caution: if the expression of love does not match the depth of the relationship, it will hurt. There will be misunderstandings, a sense of rejection, and feelings of being rashly judged. And this is very understandable because the expression is a lie. Years ago when I was first teaching at the university, one of my male students sent his girlfriend twelve dozen roses on Valentine's Day, but she returned them because they had just met. Smart girl, because twelve dozen roses did not match the depth of their relationship.

When this happens, what we're doing becomes an "act of love" that tries to show to our beloved how worthy we are of their love, or to prove to ourselves how good and loving we are, or to gain merit for ourselves in heaven. We are not loving the other person but using this person for our own gain. We try to buy the other person's love and keep them indebted to us. When this happens, it will hurt. What did my male student do when the roses came back? He got a twelve-pack of beer and got drunk.

The next stage of prayer is the stage of presence. Now love has gone deeper and words will not express the depth of love, and signs and symbols may be inadequate to communicate this love that now exists. This is the stage where love is communicated in its purity. It is here that we express and experience our deepest love for our beloved. When we have an ecstatic experience of any kind, all that we can do is absorb it in silence by just being present. No artist will paint a beautiful sunset while it is happening, because no one who is describing the sunset as it is happening is really *with* the sunset. But that which is experienced in silence will later come out in the form of a beautiful painting or a deeply felt poem.

Or think about when we are in the presence of a loved one who is dying: we can say nothing, we can do nothing, and all that we can really do is just remain fully present and fully focused on that person. And in that silent watching there is a very deep communication between us and the one we love. We communicate in the purest form without the obstacles of words or signs and symbols. In that presence and focus there is just our self and our beloved—our self and the person that we love. We are in deep communion with this loved one.

It is the same in our relationship with God. Jesus would invite people to come and see or just to watch and pray. In the experience of the transfiguration or the passion of Jesus, all that his inner circle of disciples could do was to be present and take in the mystery they were experiencing.

And in our own prayer experience we will at some point come to a place when we cannot pray our favorite prayers meaningfully and those Scripture verses that inspired and helped us so much do not have the same effect or any at all. It is at this time when we are invited in our relationship with God to go into the stage of presence. We put away our Scriptures, shut our mouths, and in silence we look at God and God looks at us. In this experience of presence we communicate deeply and are drawn into a still deeper intimacy with the Divine.

From my own personal experience and the experience of spiritually directing others I've come to believe that this stage comes with a price. There is a spiritual burning of sorts that purifies us to the core so that we can love deeply. This is what is revealed in Deuteronomy 18:16, when the people of Israel came to Moses and told him, "Let us not again hear the voice of the LORD, our God, nor see this great fire any more [which means to see his holy face], . . . lest we die." The ancient Israelites knew that listening to the voice of God or seeing the face of God was an invitation to die. We die to our false selves. When we see God face to face, it is as if God's holy fire or his Divine presence burns away all the masks we wear and all the "skins" we have put onto ourselves with which we falsely identify. The good news is that if we have the courage to enter into this stage of prayer, the stage of presence, there we receive insight into who we really are and enjoy the unbounded freedom that comes with this.

I remember my ordination retreat. We were to spend eight days in prayer. I wanted to give myself fully to this retreat and came with the best of dispositions. I gave my whole self to every exercise and every demand of this retreat. I met with my retreat director every day. The first day, he asked me how the retreat was going, and I said that I was struggling a bit, but since it was just the beginning it would be okay. But then the next day very little had changed. My director asked me a few questions and told me to carry on.

In the time that followed, each day was worse than the previous one. My director kept asking me a few questions and continued to tell me to carry on. On the sixth day I told my director that I had prayed for him the previous night. I prayed that God would put some sense into his silly head. Here I'm telling him day after day that nothing is happening in my prayer, and he just keeps insisting that I carry on. He asked his questions and once again said, "Carry on."

That night, it was about one-thirty in the morning, I was alone in the chapel after desperately trying to pray all evening, and all of a sudden I was face to face with God. Call it a vision, imagination, or a mere fantasy—whatever. What I know is that God was in my presence and I was in the presence of God. I complained to God saying that I gave my best to this retreat but could not feel God's closeness. I was tired and wanted to lay my head on God's shoulders and rest. But to my surprise God was worn out too and wanted to rest in my lap. And when I found God resting in my lap, I broke down and cried, sobbing without any control. I do not know how long this lasted, but my prayer life and my relationship with God has never been the same.

Now why did my retreat director tell me to carry on? When he asked me about my prayer, I realized that I would go into the small chapel after dinner around eight thirty at night and remain there until about four or five in the morning. All I said during that time was, "Lord, teach me to pray. . . . Lord, I believe, help my unbelief. . . . Lord, I believe, strengthen my faith." And my favorite prayer was, "My soul is thirsting for the Lord. When shall I see you face to face? I want to see you face to face." And so on the sixth day of the retreat at one-thirty in the morning, God was face to face with me! This then is the prayer of presence.

The fourth stage of a relationship is to experience a presence in absence. This is when the lover and the beloved become two in one flesh. You do not really need the physical presence of your beloved, but whatever happens to you, you are never alone. Something good happens to you, you have your beloved to share it with. Something painful happens to you, you always have a shoulder to lean on, even though your beloved might be a thousand miles away. This stage of a relationship is easy to understand when someone very close to you dies or goes away. That person becomes more alive now than when the person was with you and living.

I remember my dad. After my mother died he would go every day to her grave and pray the rosary. He would then spend time having a heart-to-heart conversation with her. At home he often talked to her, and it was as if she was always there. One day he shared with me what he was doing and asked if he was going crazy. I told him that even though mom was gone physically she was present to him in a very real way. This went on for many years, and then one day my dad said that he saw mom come in the front door. She looked very beautiful and had a very pretty dress on. She had a beautiful smile and she said to him, "I am very happy and I want you to be happy too." He never saw her again. He did not need to see her again. My father was sure he now had mom with him forever.

In our relationship with God, we too become two in one flesh with God. It is at this stage of the relationship that we do not have to go to a sacred mountain or a temple to experience God. God is spirit and truth and can be experienced in the cave of our hearts because God and I have become one. And now everything that I do is prayer, because all that I do is through this relationship, which is growing ever deeper and ever greater.

The Third Paradigm: Mind, Heart, and Consciousness

There is one more way of deepening my romance with the Divine through prayer. It is through the prayer of the mind, the prayer of the heart, and the prayer of consciousness.

God does draw a person into a relationship through a person's mind. A person reflects on the Scriptures, on spiritual writings, on life experiences, on the social sciences and pure sciences and then formulates a philosophy or a theology. This way of encountering God I call the prayer of the mind.

One popular way of applying this prayer is to take a Scripture passage and reflect on it. Let's take the story of Bartimaeus, the blind man in Mark's Gospel (10:46–52). To use this method we read the passage a couple of times, and then answer a few questions:

1. **"What word or phrase stood out for me?"** Write this word or phrase down.

2. **"Is there a person or a group with whom I identify closely right now, and what are the reasons for this?"** For example, am I like the blind man, who cries out for help? Or perhaps I identify with the ones close to Jesus who ask the blind man to be quiet and in a way keep him from spiritual help? Or am I like the ones who come and bring the blind man to the most effective help? Or perhaps I feel like Jesus, who goes about helping those in need? Reflect on this and write down your responses.

3. **Look into your life and find areas that need healing.** Make a list.

4. **Write down or compose a prayer asking God to help you.** Pray this prayer, aloud or in silence.

We can use this method to reflect on anything in life. Through this method we receive revelations about ourselves and God, and we make resolutions to become a better person. We formulate or amend our personal philosophies or theology. Our prayer at the end is characterized mostly by petitions, asking or begging even for something from God. The prayer of the mind is a good and valid way of praying, but there are others.

The prayer of the heart is where God is revealed to us through our feelings, and our prayer is one of appreciation and gratitude for the gifts and blessings we receive. In this way of praying we open ourselves to the mystery of God and the mystery of life and allow that mystery to fill us and transform us into the very mystery we are praying about. In the East we believe that you always become what your heart is open to—so if you open yourself to a stone you will become just like a stone, if you open yourself to a river, you will become like a river—any part of creation you open yourself to, that is what you will become. And if you open yourself to God, you will discover your identity in the Divine. When we open ourselves to the mystery of life, then life will take us beyond our present boundaries to newer and infinite horizons. Then our prayer becomes one of appreciation, gratitude, and love.

Feelings are more authentic than a multitude of thoughts, philosophies, or theologies. Carl Jung once described reality as that which affects us. God becomes more and more real as we allow God to affect us on an ever-deeper level of our being. Our experience of our prayers of the heart become our rule of life, our reality, even if they sometimes contradict sacred laws, mores, or long-standing traditions.

A method for this type of prayer is to focus on the heart of the mystery we open ourselves to—if it is a person we admire, we focus on the heart of this person during both times of joy and experiences of pain. We make the heart and spirit of this person our own. For example, one of my very close friends, A. T. Thomas, was tortured and beheaded while he was working to empower a group of people in northern India. When I think of the way this friend of mine was tortured and the pain he endured, I feel hopeless and terribly afraid. But then I focus on the heart and spirit of this man, and I feel that with his spirit and his heart I can go through any pain. Such an experience is my prayer of the heart.

The third kind of prayer in this paradigm is the prayer of consciousness. I will explain it to you in the Eastern way. In the East we worship the cobra and in the Eastern tradition we do not allow this snake to sleep. You always wake up the cobra, so that it is always active and potent. Now, when you are in the presence of a striking cobra, with its gaze focused on you and it able to kill you at any moment—that is the prayer of consciousness. In the presence of a striking cobra you are fully awake, you are fully alive, all your senses are present to this cobra. You are fully "I," fully "now," and fully "here."

In the prayer of consciousness you are the *I* not the *me*. What is the *I*? The *I* is the breath of God. The *I* is the image and likeness of God. The *I* is the divine in you. In the presence of the striking cobra, you are not thinking about the *me*. You are not thinking about all the stupid things you did in your life—you may be killed if you do. You are not thinking about all the naughty or nasty things that you have done— you will die. You are not even thinking of all the good things that you have done in your life; if you do, you also will die. What about all the material things in your life? They are all a part of the *me*. And the things that people say or think about you? Also part of the *me* and can distract you from the cobra and get you killed. The power and authority that you had in your life—that you believed gave you your identity—will not make a difference in the present situation. You discover and experience your true and only identity, the *I* that is the image and likeness of God or the breath of the Divine.

All that you are conscious of before a striking cobra is the situation you are in, and you are fully present to that moment. Then you are fully in the *now*. You are not thinking about the past or the future. There will be no past or future if you are distracted. You are fully in the *now*. You experience the Divine identity that God revealed to Moses, "I am." When you are fully present to the now, you are living and experiencing eternal time. Why? Because this moment now is part of every moment from the beginning of time; this moment now is part of every moment till the end of time. This moment now is eternal time.

And then you are fully *here*. If in the presence of the cobra you would rather be somewhere else, this desire would take your focus away from the present situation and moment, and you would certainly die. Now if I am fully here, then this place is a part of everywhere and so I too am a part of everywhere. Just as right now, this here—the chair that you are sitting on and the ground that your feet are on—is part of everywhere.

So this prayer of consciousness is being fully *I*, fully *now*, fully *here*. This prayer of consciousness is a way of life. Anytime I am fully present to anything it is my prayer. The situation does not have to be religious. Every mundane activity that draws our full attention is prayer.

Another way of looking at this is to live every moment and to do everything as if it were the first time, the last time, or the only time we would be doing it. When you eat, eat as if you are eating for the first time, the last time, and the only time, and you will be a mystic. When you eat something for the first time, you are so present to the food. You eat slowly and pay attention to the taste and how the food feels in your mouth. You are curious about the ingredients. If for some reason this particular meal is going to be your last one—your last steak or last dessert—you will make sure you enjoy every morsel of it, and you will want to make it last. And if this is your only meal, you know you will eat it differently. Nothing else will really matter to you while you are eating. Your food gets your full attention. Your eating experience then is a mystical one. When you are eating as if you are eating for the first time, the last time, and the only time, you will experience the fullness of life. You can have the same experience when you meet people—meet them as if you were meeting them for the first time, the last time, and the only time. When you are with your children, when you are with your family, experience them with the freshness of that first time, last time, and only time. Your experience of them then becomes a prayer of consciousness, and you will be a mystic! Try this in every situation of your day and every moment of your life.

We have a poignant story in India about a man who was chased by a tiger. He runs as fast as he can and jumps into a well to escape the tiger. As he falls he lands on a branch of a tree. While he is safely perched on the branch, he looks up and sees the tiger waiting for him at the top of the well. He looks down and sees at the bottom writhing poisonous snakes. He looks around him and, as it is fruit season, sees that the tree is loaded with ripe fruit. He reaches out and begins to eat the tasty, juicy fruit. Now think about this. Just because there is a tiger waiting at the top and poisonous snakes at the bottom, why should the man deprive himself of the beauty and the gift of the moment?

Sometimes in our lives there are tigers and snakes waiting for us at home, at school, or at work. We obsess about them, worry about them, and let them take control of our lives. How often when we actually encountered these tigers or snakes did they have a change of heart or were not as bad as we thought, and then we wonder why we did not enjoy all the good and exciting things our day had to offer? And what if those tigers or snakes decide to eat us? We still have a choice: to be eaten having enjoyed the fruit of the day or not having enjoyed everything the day had to offer us.

Now think about how many moments of your day are actual negative events or situations and the tension associated with the experience? The rest of our bad feelings in any given day are the guilt that we carry over from the past or fear and anxiety of the future. So if we do live every moment as the *I-now-here*, without fretting over the past or future, we would be free of these bad feelings. We would live not only spiritual lives but healthy psychological and emotional lives as well.

So the prayer of consciousness—being fully *I*, fully *now*, fully *here*—is a way of life, a way of living our true divine identity, which turns all that we do into prayer.

18

Finding Your Identity, Encountering God

You can't really romance God, or anyone else, if you haven't yet found yourself. If you don't know yourself and don't love yourself, how can you be in a loving relationship with God? You are not bringing yourself into the relationship. It's one-sided. You, the authentic you, needs to be there in the relationship—you need to come to the table and share in the feast. Then you can commune. Then you can share love.

So what is our true identity? Well, we have to find it to experience it ourselves. But the Bible sheds light on this right from the start. This matter is so important that the Bible starts out with this. In the first two chapters of the book of Genesis we see that we are made in the image and likeness of God, who breathed God's own life into humanity. In the third chapter we are told that skins were put onto us and we lost sight and experience of our true selves. For the whole of our lives we are trying to go beyond the skins that differentiate us as "Jew or Greek, slave or free, male or female" and regain our real identity.

This reminds me of a story of an ornithologist who once found an eagle in a chicken yard. He talked to the farmer and asked him what the king of all birds was doing among those chickens. The farmer politely told him that he had found the eagle as a little baby and had put it with the chickens to see if it would survive. The chickens did not have any problem accepting the eagle, and in fact they did not even notice the difference. The little eagle grew up feeling so much at home with the chickens that it believed that it was just like all the other chickens. It ate like them and even cackled like them.

The ornithologist asked the farmer to give him a chance to free the eagle, and so he took the eagle in his hand and talked to it about how it was the king of all the birds and that its place was in the sky and not the chicken yard. The eagle cackled and went right back to the other chickens and fought to get its food. The following day the ornithologist came again and took the eagle to a rooftop and tried to talk about the identity of the eagle, but the sound and sight of the other chickens drew the eagle back to the chicken coop.

But this lover of birds did not give up and came early one morning long before daybreak and took the eagle onto a high mountain. As the first rays of the rising sun hit the eye of the eagle, all of a sudden something shifted in its soul. It gave one shrill cry, spread its wings, and flew out into the wide-open sky. The eagle had found its identity. It was actually the king of all the birds.

If you find your true self, you will love yourself. And if you love yourself, you will find your true self. They go

together. And in the finding of yourself and loving of yourself, you will experience the Divine. We cannot love God and
relate with the Divine if we do not recognize our identity as
children of God and live like Divine heirs. But once we do,
then as heirs, all that is God's is at our disposal. Everything in
the universe, known and unknown, becomes a revelation of
the Divine and speaks of God to us.

This is like the story of the Zen master who shared
with his disciples that before his enlightenment he was
depressed. After his enlightenment, he said, he continued to
be depressed. What is the difference then? Before enlightenment, he identified himself with his depression. Afterward,
he did not. It is like the sky and the clouds: Before enlightenment he identified with the clouds—the dark depressing ones
and the bright joyful ones. After enlightenment he felt like
the sky and watched the clouds roll by without any of them
becoming part of his identity. He does not change, his depression does not change, but he recognizes and lives his greater
identity, beyond and in spite of himself.

19

Getting Better and Better, Doing the Same Thing

I was born into a very Catholic family. We were initiated into the Catholic tradition with tremendous fear and guilt. We kept the commandments of the church and those that the priest preached from the pulpit. We observed the ritual and had many family and neighborhood devotions. We took pride in calling ourselves Roman Catholics.

Then when I was twelve years old, we moved from the Catholic ghetto in which we had lived into a multireligious area. We were one of four Christian families among two hundred other non-Christian families. Most of them were Hindus, some Muslims, some Zoroastrians, and even a few Jewish families. Moving away from the Catholic ghetto into this non-Christian environment exposed me to new experiences and expanded my spiritual search. Spurred by my father's questioning and my mother's spirit of exploring new possibilities, my family began to see ourselves as Indian Christians.

Even though we continued all the Catholic practices we had followed in our previous home, for some reason something seemed to be changing from within us. As Indian Christians now we began to shed our Catholic guilt and anxiety. We emulated the spirit of those we now lived with. We learned to see ourselves as spiritual and celebrated our divine connection.

In one sense nothing had changed and yet in a very real way everything had changed. When I was young, we would say a family rosary—and half the time my father was making sure we were attentive to our prayer because my siblings and I would either be sleeping or were distracted. But my father prayed the rosary with my mother to the end of their lives. From the beginning to the end of his life, my father prayed the rosary. His rosary was worn out—those beads were worn out by just his holding them every day. In the beginning, it was the words and the rituals that were important. Later, the mysteries that he prayed about drew his attention. That was what he would focus on in his prayer. Then, toward the end of his life, praying the rosary created an atmosphere of the mystical and the divine. The words were no longer important. Neither were the mysteries that he prayed about.

In a sense, he prayed the same prayer all his life, and yet the effect was vastly different. Even though he was faithful to the daily recitation of the rosary, his whole day was lived in the presence and awareness of God; the divine milieu during the time of the rosary overflowed into the rest of his day. When my father prayed the rosary during the last six or seven years of his life, he was in a mystical mode. He said the words; everything seemed the same, and yet everything had changed. Because when my father prayed the rosary, you just looked at him and sensed that he was somewhere else, in another world, a world of the mystical and the Divine. His relationship with God had deepened and deepened over the years through this same prayer. My father was doing the same thing he always did, but getting better and better while doing it.

Similarly, in the beginning my father would attend Mass every day because it made him feel good. Mass, like all his other religious practices, helped him avoid going to hell. He accumulated merit for when he died and showed up before the throne of God. Later, even though he kept up his same pious practices, he did so not so much to avoid hell but because they helped him make contact with God and deepen his relationship with the Divine.

In the beginning, my dad would only go to communion on Sundays after making his confession on the previous day. Later, he would go to communion every time he attended the Eucharist. Toward the end of his life, it became less important to him to attend church. Neither did he feel the need to go to confession. God was very real to him now, and he had found his confidence and freedom in the loving relationship he had developed with the Divine.

My father was always living life on an ever-deeper level. My sister tried for many years before he died to take him to church just in case he wanted to make his confession, but he didn't want to go. What would he have to confess? He did not have a negative thought about anyone or anything.

This theme also defined our family experience. When we moved from the Catholic ghetto and lived in the religiously diverse area, in some ways nothing had changed. We did all the same things. Our family routine was the same. So in one sense, nothing had changed. But in another sense, everything had changed. Somehow moving from that Catholic ghetto into this non-Christian environment exposed us to a greater experience and new possibilities in our spiritual journey. We had the courage to go beyond sacred boundaries and seek new horizons. What we learned from our non-Christian neighbors was that religion was a celebration of life, not just a means to avoid hell. We were introduced to a variety of ways of experiencing God and deepening our relationship with the Divine. Religion slowly became a way of life rather than a series of do's and don'ts. Our family continued the same Catholic practices but with a different attitude and meaning. Our lives were the same, but in this new context, this new milieu, everything had changed, and all our experiences had somehow deepened.

The morning my dad died, I wasn't home. He died in the presence of my siblings. He was eighty-six years old. He kept asking, "Is Paul coming back? Does he know I'm not well?" And they said, yes, he'll be back—but they didn't expect him to die because my dad wasn't sick or bedridden. He had fainted that morning and felt uneasy. The family physician was brought in and prescribed some drugs. But then about three-thirty in the afternoon he began to say, "I don't think I'm going to get well again." He pulled his hand away from my sister, made the sign of the cross, looked at all of them,

20

No Law above the Law of Love

After a person has had a Divine desert experience and found their true identity, that person will experience life differently. Jesus, for example, broke the Jewish Sabbath because after his desert experience he lived life following a different law. He lived totally by God's law—the Law of Love. He's in love with the Divine. He's in it and there is nothing else.

Today we've gotten used to the idea that Jesus broke the Sabbath. He did things on that sacred day in Jewish culture that were forbidden in that tradition to do. We have to remind ourselves what that really meant back then. I think you couldn't have done something worse in that society at the time than break the law of the Sabbath. It was considered so sacred, to break the Sabbath was scandalous! And yet Jesus does it again and again and again. Because he's drawn into something that is even greater, something that is better, something beyond any other law—he's in love with God and now governed solely by this relationship and the Law of Love.

And so we see Jesus consistently break many of the social norms. He moved around with women and even talked to women in public, which was not allowed by the ancient Jewish law. Jewish society at the time was patriarchal, and if you were a holy man, you didn't mix with women. One can imagine the Pharisee getting up in the morning and saying, "I thank you, God, for making me a man and not a woman." And here's Jesus going around spending his time with women. And not just *any* women; he spends time with the Samaritans. He also spends his time with prostitutes, tax collectors, and sinners. Because he doesn't care about being "good" for society or even being "good" for God; he's living life differently now, following the Law of Love. So after Jesus' desert experience, nothing has changed and yet everything has changed.

Paul did the same thing. Before his desert experience, Paul lived life according to the Mosaic law and followed what was good and proper—and he was fighting God. He was fighting all those who were in love with God and who were following "the Way" that Jesus taught. Paul once wrote that "if he should find any men or women who belonged to the Way, he would bring them back to Jerusalem in chains." Then Paul had his Damascus experience, this intense encounter with the Divine, and he threw the Mosaic law out the window. He's got a new law: "in Christ Jesus, there is neither Jew nor Greek, there is neither slave nor free person, there is not male and female" (Galatians 3:28). Now Paul breaks the Mosaic law that he once held so highly and embraces God's Law of Love.

He goes against circumcision. He fights against the Judaizers who want all new Christians to be circumcised before they are baptized in order that they become Jews before they become Christians. Even though circumcision back then was *the* mark of belonging to the people of God, Paul fights the Judaizers. He instead talks about a circumcision of the heart rather than of the body. So now the mark of this bond, this covenant with God, is in your heart. It is expressed in the life of freedom driven only by the spirit of God and not any external law. You carry that mark within yourself. Paul could do this because he was seeing life differently, following the Law of Love. So for Paul, too, nothing in his life had changed and yet everything had changed.

St. Ignatius's case is the same. After his desert experience in Manresa, he lived life by a new law. When he formed the Jesuits, he put things into the order's constitutions that went against the teaching and practices of the Catholic Church of his time. For example, the essential part of any Catholic order's community life then was to pray the Office, which was the prayer of the church, together—and he threw that right out. Other basic characteristics of religious life back then were to have penance by law, to remain together as a community, and to spend a set time in prayer every day. But Ignatius had other priorities. The only law he gave to a Jesuit who had completed the order's formation process was the law of charity and love. That's it. Follow the law of charity and love that the Spirit engraves on the hearts of every individual. Every other type of law or precept or social structure was now irrelevant to Ignatius. When his Jesuit companions would get nervous and challenge him about this, saying, "How can you do this? Do you know what you are doing?" Ignatius would simply answer: "I saw it at Manresa." For him, nothing had changed and yet everything had changed.

Because of their desert experiences, Jesus, Paul, and Ignatius had a new law, a new way of living. They found an absolute in their relationship with the Divine, and all else was now relative and subject to ever deeper experience of that Divine. So the structures of society—and even religion—they were good, but did not reign supreme.

Now I'm not saying that all the laws of church and society and culture are bad. Most of these laws at one time sprang from someone's personal experience of the Divine, someone who was likely in love with God. And that law was their personal response to being in love with the Divine; it was how they lived life differently at that time. But later others took that response and made it a tradition or a law, even though these people had never had the Divine experience from which this response had blossomed. They did not understand it in spirit—how it resonated with God's law. And then some of these people enforced this "law" upon others. For Jesus or for Paul or for Ignatius it would have been an insincere decision to adopt someone else's laws of living when these did not come from or harmonize with their own experience of the Divine. Because they had been seduced by God into the desert and had come out with a more intimate understanding and love of God, they were changed.

One of the more challenging questions we should ask ourselves is this: how many laws are we ready to break because we love God? Sacred laws, holy laws, divine laws. If you truly love God and are looking for the bigger life, the better life, then you and I at some point will be called to break laws that are very sacred. Because after our own desert experience, with a new vision of the Divine, of ourselves, and of life, we too will be changed and have to live life differently. That's what it means to be governed by the Law of Love. That's what happens when you are romancing the Divine.

21

Love, and Do What You Want

Mistakes are a part of life. And a person who has fallen in love will make plenty of mistakes. But the Law of Love allows us to make mistakes—because whatever we've done, it was done in love.

I like to tell parents, "We all have the right to mess up the lives of our children." We never do it like our parents did to us; we do it our own way. We think we know what is good for them, how it's all supposed to be. So because we love our children, we mess up their lives. And yet, at the end of the day, we will look back and say, "Well, what I did, I did out of love. I was ignorant. I didn't know any better. But what I did, I did out of love."

Sometimes I hear fathers say that they hate the parable of the prodigal son because it is unfair to the older son. Is it not right and just, they ask, that fathers should expect their children to obey and respect them? And then I ask these fathers what they would prefer from their children: to be respected or to be loved? I respected my parents very much and loved them, too, but I did not always obey their wishes. My mother never wanted me to be a priest. I went against her deepest desires and plans for me, but that doesn't mean that I loved her any less or did not respect her. On the contrary, because of our mutual love and respect I could disobey her and my father.

The other thing that I try to tell parents is that they cannot be responsible for their children forever. Once the children grow up to be adults they need to take responsibility for their own lives and make of it what they sincerely want. One of my students once said to me, "I am like this because my father was an alcoholic." And my spontaneous response to this young man was, "Perhaps your father took to drinking after you were born." Making our parents scapegoats for the mess of our adult lives is certainly not healthy.

When a person following the Law of Love makes a mistake, there is no need for that person to blame, shame, or punish themselves. Instead, the person can admit their error and learn from their mistake, without all that negativity. Because following the Law of Love doesn't require you to be perfect; it only requires your sincerity.

We often fail to understand or forget that God doesn't care about our imperfections—all God cares about is *you*.

There was once a young man who wanted to pluck all the stars from the sky. So he goes and he plucks and he plucks and he plucks. The more stars he plucks, the more stars appear in the sky, and sometimes the ones he had plucked go back into the sky. So in his frustration he goes to his teacher, his guru, and says, "What should I do?" And the master calmly advises him, "Wait until the sun comes up." So he waits and the sun comes up and it is shining so bright. And suddenly the man realizes the

stars are still there—they haven't disappeared from the sky—
but when the sun shines so bright, you can hardly notice them.

We spend so much energy trying to pluck our mistakes
and imperfections out of our lives. But when the sunshine of
God's love and God's life is radiating so bright in our lives,
we remain aware of our sins but can hardly notice them. If
we only spent the same energy giving God's love a chance to
begin shining in our hearts and in our lives, life would be so
beautiful. Life would be so wonderful. There's no room for
shame, guilt, and self-punishment in the face of all that love.

So following the Law of Love, sincere in our hearts,
allows us to make mistakes and have imperfections. We need
to free ourselves from the idea that we have to be perfect or else
we've ruined our chances with God. In the first place, we don't
know what "perfect" really is. St. John writes that if we say we
are without sin, we make God a liar (1 John 1:10). And in the
Taoist tradition, the *Tao Te Ching* says, "The saint is not flawed
because he knows he is flawed." We are meant to get our hands
dirty in the clay of brokenness, weakness, and imperfection
now and then. The second chapter of Genesis tells us that God
was playing with clay and with God's own hands formed man
and woman, and breathed into humanity the Divine breath of
life. Clay means weakness—that which has no structure, no
integrity of its own, only what the master craftsman makes of
it. So in our weakness, the Divine life manifests. Dwelling too
much on trying to be perfect and not allowing God to filter
through our brokenness—that would be the sin.

I believe this is what frees us to live outside of tradition
and mores and to break sacred laws in order to experience life
to the fullest.

22

Loving God, a Way of Life

Once, an exercise was given to a group of older people. They were told to imagine themselves in a place they loved. Relaxed and happy, lost in enjoying beautiful surroundings . . . and all of a sudden you see Jesus coming up to you. What would you do? One lady had seen herself on a beach, sitting in a rocking chair. She was lost in enjoyment of the sea breeze, and the sight and sound of the gentle, rhythmic waves below a beautiful sky. The crying of the seagulls added to the music of the sea. She rocked herself happy. But when Jesus came up to her, the woman saw herself jump out of the chair and get immediately on her knees. Her response was to worship Jesus as she had been taught all her life. What happened to the beautiful scene? All that she had been enjoying just disappeared. Was she still happy once Jesus arrived? She didn't know—her face was to the sand. It was as if Jesus' arrival had thrown a wet blanket on her whole experience. If you were in this situation, what would you sincerely do? Would you react similarly to this lady? Would you perhaps invite Jesus to share with you the beautiful moment instead of letting it slip away? Or would your experience of God be one more everyday experience?

Loving God is a way of life. We grow in our relationship with God here and now. God is present and here for us now—right here, this moment, for you and me. As I write this book, God is inviting me to renew some of the experiences, gifts, and graces I've been given and to open myself to discover new experiences and deeper gifts and graces as I interact with you. The same is true for you as you engage in the activity of reading this. At this very moment, there exists an invitation from God to encounter and grow in your relationship with the Divine. Whether you agree or disagree with what I've written, whether you are experiencing positive or negative reactions to my words, your reading of this book can be a form of prayer. Prayer is an action. God is present and if you are with God in love as you read this, then you are experiencing prayer in action.

The action of prayer is in the ordinariness of our daily lives; it is encountering God in that everyday moment. Think about it—if we don't encounter God in what we're doing now, how are we going to encounter God in what we're not doing later? Another way to understand this is to imagine you are sitting down at a table eating a wonderful steak. An angel comes and tells you that in fifteen minutes you are going to die. So here you are sitting with a delicious, juicy steak and you are going to die. What do you do? Continue eating? Because it is in eating the steak that you will experience God and find your communion with the Divine. Of course, it's easy to say that but harder to sincerely do it—unless we've made prayer in action our way of life and our pathway to union and communion with the Divine. I like Woody Allen's contemplation on death: "It's not that I'm afraid to die, I just don't want to be there when it happens." That is honesty. But our goal as lovers of God is to be able to sincerely continue eating the steak, being in the moment, aware of God's presence, and experiencing the Divine in our every daily act.

I am also reminded of another story about an angel who appeared to a real baseball fanatic. The angel was describing how wonderful heaven was, but the baseball fanatic was only interested if they played baseball in heaven. The angel replied, "We have great baseball parks and really great games. And guess what? You're pitching tomorrow night!"

Now if the angel said that to us, would we be ready to pitch tomorrow? If we have been living prayer in action, we probably would.

Sometimes we may have the opposite experience. I tell my students, if you attend Mass and have all this lively song and great liturgy but you haven't seen the face of God—you have wasted your time in church. You could have had a better time going to the symphony, going to a party, or going to a bar—there you can have even more exciting times. How do we know when we have seen the face of God? By the effect. When the Divine has touched us, we feel different. Just like when we fall in love—we know that it has happened because we feel changed. So if we do not see the face of God at church, then our attending was not prayer in action. We did not deepen our relationship with the Divine.

3

Being in Love
with God

23

Being in Love with the Divine

Once there was a caterpillar. It was unattractive, crawled everywhere, and ate dirt. One day, it was drawn into a cocoon, and with courage entered a dark and seemingly hopeless world. Slowly, almost imperceptibly, it began to transform and change, finally emerging as a beautiful butterfly. Now this former caterpillar can fly. It can sit on thorns and is not affected by those things that could hurt it before, but instead makes the thorns look more beautiful. And it can rest on the flowers and not be affected by those either, but makes these beautiful things in life even more attractive. The butterfly is free. It just is—it's just living its life. It has to prove its goodness and its beauty to no one.

This is what it is like for a person who has come to the state of being in love with the Divine. When we are in love with the Divine, we do not have to prove our love or do anything to earn love. We just are *in love*. We are very much like the butterfly: our romance with the Divine begins with an attraction or a seduction that pulls us into a desert experience; the caterpillar's cocoon is in a very real way its desert or cave experience. We, too, need to have the courage to take the risk of entering into the cocoon and being lost forever. God may seem far away in these times of transition and growth. In fact, just as the caterpillar has to struggle by its own power to break free of the cocoon, we too have to find our own inner strength and power to break forth from the obstacles and barriers that try to contain our true selves. Once we have had our desert experience and have been purified and transformed, we attain the freedom of the butterfly and begin to live the fullness of life. Loving the Divine, we can find meaning and strength in the thorns of our lives and celebrate the roses without clinging to those either. Like the butterfly, we learn to flow with life, we become part of the flow of life; we allow life to happen to us.

It is important that we all come to understand one thing: while we may have to struggle through periods of growth and purification in the desert to reach the place where we can experience love, it's not an effort to be in love. Love happens. When we have to work to be in love—*I'm going to make myself be in love with someone, make myself a great lover of this person*—that's not being in love. Love isn't something that we make happen—it's something that we just discover because it's there, we are there. It's like opening our eyes and all of a sudden realizing we *are* in love.

It's the same with being in love with the Divine. There is not a strategy for being in love with God. It's not an exercise to do. It cannot be "studied" or "learned" or "practiced" in the traditional sense. There aren't "ten easy steps" for this. And although I can tell you a lot about the process leading up to it, I cannot tell you *how* to be in love with God—no one can.

But we can explore together what it looks like, I can share a little about what it feels like, and we can reflect on stories that reveal what happened to others who have—totally, completely, and irrevocably—surrendered themselves into love with the Divine. Jesus throughout his ministry was constantly trying to teach people what the kingdom of God was like. He couldn't just put people there or make them understand. So he used parable after parable to try to express this.

Here, in these last few chapters, we will take a similar approach. Through story, analogy, and personal experience, I would like to provide some landmarks for the terrain ahead and signposts to help guide us on our journey of love. I'll try to describe what happens to a person when he or she is in love with God. What does being in love with the Divine look like? And where does that take us? Let's begin.

Being in love with the Divine is like the story of Michelangelo, who once went to buy some marble for one of his masterpieces. He came to this shop and saw a piece lying in a corner. He was gripped by this abandoned piece. The shopkeeper was surprised and apologized for not throwing that old broken piece out long ago. It had been lying there forgotten and collecting dust for some time. But Michelangelo insisted that he have it, and when the shopkeeper wanted to know why, Michelangelo simply said that there was an angel hidden in it and he wanted to set it free. There is an angel hidden in each of us waiting to be free. There are angels hidden everywhere, waiting for Michelangelos like us to recognize them and to set them free.

Being in love with the Divine is also illustrated for us by the famous story of the frog prince. A prince is put under a spell that makes him a frog. The prince never loses sight of his personal identity; even as a frog, he knew he was a prince. A lovely young princess encounters the frog in the woods and accepts him as her beloved companion. For three days and three nights she took this little frog everywhere she went—in her playroom, her dining table, and even her own bed. After enjoying three days of her presence and love, the prince blossoms once again into his true identity and regains his freedom. As soon as the spell is broken the prince marries this princess and they live happily ever after. Now, if the prince did not see himself as a prince, he would have perhaps lived and died as a frog. And would he have been able to live his true identity if the lovely princess had not loved him?

Jesus also picked lowly, grubby people for his disciples and companions. He loved them and gave them back their identities as sons and daughters of God. With that dignity they were able to live free and happy lives. He went to the social and religious outcasts and invited them to the full meaning of their lives. If they accepted his gift, they were changed for the rest of their lives.

Often society and religion keep us as frogs as long as they can. They insist that we are born sinners, live like hopeless sinners, and die in the state of sin. We get little hope or encouragement to change and find our dignity and our true identity. Our inner freedom becomes a threat to the powers that be. But God continually comes to us through people and life experiences, revealing to us who God is and who we are in our relationship with the Divine. Every now and then we find some prince or princess who believes in us and who through love helps us recognize and experience who we truly are—children of God and divine heirs.

24

Letting Go

Many of us have heard and often sung that famous song "On Eagle's Wings" in church. As we sing the words of this lovely song we can almost feel ourselves being carried up by God on divine wings. It feels so safe and so good that we wish this divine ride might never end—but it does. Because in reality, our spiritual ride on eagle's wings is not a joyride but an invitation to let ourselves be dropped into nothingness. When this happens, those who try to grasp and cling to the divine wings that had carried them are clinging to an illusion—they're not the ones who will one day end up in love with God. Those who get angry at the Divine for dropping them won't find themselves in the state of being in love either. The ones who will someday find themselves wholly and definitively in love with the Divine are the ones who let go and let themselves fall.

Let me explain.

One of my favorite symbols is the eagle. I have spent many hours of my life watching eagles. I love the freedom and the ease with which eagles scan the sky, and from their perspective, I would imagine a mountain of a problem looks but a molehill. The reality of life is much more expansive from the eagle's view.

I was reading one time about the eagle and how it builds its nest in the high mountains on a cliff—a big beautiful nest—and there it lays its eggs. There it hatches its young ones. And in those clean, clear heights the young ones grow from being little baby eaglets, feeling comfortable and secure in that big nest while the male eagle fiercely guards the nest from any predators. The eaglets have this warm and close relationship with the mother eagle. They have a great time together until all of a sudden one day, the mother eagle begins to push them out of the nest, and when they resist, she begins to get rid of the soft, fluffy bed that they were so accustomed to. Underneath there are thorns and thistles. The little eaglets wonder, what's going on? The mother eagle continues to break the nest bit by bit, twig by twig, until soon the little ones all fall out and drop into nothingness. And as they drop, the mother eagle swoops down and picks them up on her wings—to save them, right? No. She takes them up to an even higher place and drops them again. And then, to an even higher place, to be dropped again. Until the eagles can spread their own wings, find their own strength, and make the sky their home.

In our spiritual journey, we too will be pushed out of our comfortable nests and dropped into nothingness to find out what we are capable of and to be transformed. If we have any hope of being in love with the Divine, here's fair warning: we have to be willing to take the fall. It's all about letting go.

There are people in this world—some very good people—who don't really want to be in love with God. God may be important to them—they may want to please God, they may even want to serve God—but they don't want to go through what it means to be in love with God. Because that means letting go. It's a risk. It's scary. And one's sense of self, the clingy ego, wants to pull back and stay with what is safe and manageable. This false self knows that to fall in love with God means it will have to die. And so many people would rather resist change and stay with the nice, with the comfortable, with the familiar, and with just being good. These are people who do not understand the magical power of letting go at God's invitation. They will remain with their false sense of self, and their relationship with God will slowly deteriorate.

It's like the man who fell off the cliff and managed to grab onto a branch as he was falling. He called out to God to help him. God responded to him by saying that if he believed that God could save him he should let go of those roots. The man looked down and the ground was hundreds of feet below. God invites us to let go.

Consider the Bible story of the rich young man. This rich young man—a good man—meets Jesus, and Jesus looks at him with great affection. The rich young man asks Jesus, "Good teacher, what must I do to gain eternal life?" And Jesus answers, "Keep God's commandments." The rich young man replies, "I've kept the commandments ever since I was a child. I never broke any one of them. I've lived a good life." And Jesus says, "One thing is lacking. Go, sell all that you have, give it to the poor, and come, follow me." Jesus was inviting the young man into that which is better, that which is greater. But it was a risk. Give up everything, leave everything, and you might be left with nothing—right? Like the rich young man, we often decide to stay where we are. Jesus looked at this good, rich young man with great sadness, because the man had pulled back and chosen to live the good life instead of reaching for the better life. He was no longer there *in* the relationship with the Divine, ready to go forward into greater intimacy and love when God's invitation came.

So the freedom comes with letting go, the better life comes with giving up, and real life comes with dying. It's like pruning a plant: a good gardener cuts away at a plant, removing all the deadwood and wayward branches, because although it may seem like those branches are a part of the plant, they are actually dead weight, a burden. You reduce and reduce and reduce—until you are left with only that which is fully alive, fully regenerative. And thus the plant keeps growing. Let go and you'll keep growing, too.

25

Make Gratitude Your Personal Attitude

Paul's first letter to the Thessalonians was the first piece that was written in the New Testament. Paul wrote it even before the first Gospel was written, and in it he gives us his recipe for happiness and how to live in love with the Divine. His recipe is to be happy and joyful always, and the way to do this is to pray at all times. To achieve this seemingly impossible task, Paul says, one must be grateful in all circumstances.

When gratitude becomes our way of life and our inner attitude, then we will always look for something to be grateful for. And so for those who are in love with God and are grateful, bad things can never happen to them. They will see the gift in negative things that happen, and this experience will bring out the best in them. They are able to realize the more real things in life and see life for what it really is and not the passing illusions that cause so much suffering and take away our joys and happiness. When we focus with grateful hearts on the positive things in life, we find that these parts of our lives keep growing, and then we have more and more things to be grateful for.

Here is a story that illustrates this idea in a telling way. There was a young man who spent all his life taking care of anyone in need. He helped people bring peace to their families, he found jobs for people so they could live more comfortable and decent lives, he visited people in hospitals and prisons, giving them hope. In short, he was a man for others in a very real sense of the word.

But one day when occupation troops took over his little town, they arrested him on the streets and began dragging him to prison. He asked them to let him go home and tell his family he was being taken to prison, but they would not listen. Then he begged them to send a message to his family, but they dragged him away and locked him up in a high tower. The man could not stop thinking of his family, who would be anxious and worried when he did not return, and they had no way of knowing what had happened to him. He looked out the window and saw people walking down the streets, people who knew him, people whom he had helped. If only he could attract their attention, he knew that they would get a message to his wife and family, who would be more at peace.

All of a sudden he realized that he had two coins in his pocket. He took one of those in his hands, said a little prayer, and when a group of people was passing under his window, he threw it right in the midst of them. He was sure that if one of them saw that coin, they would look up and see him. He dropped the first coin to the ground, and yes, a young man saw the coin and picked it up. But the young man did not look up—he just said, "My lucky day," put the coin into his pocket, and walked away. The man had one more coin. With all the hope in his heart he threw the second coin right into the midst of another group that was walking by. A lady ran after this coin and picked it up. She was so happy. "My lucky day!" she said, put it into her pocket, and skipped away.

The man was sad and in his desperation began to stare around at the walls of his cell. It was an old dilapidated room. He noticed some loose powder and displaced bricks. He flung these at the next group that was passing by—and this time all of them looked up!

God is constantly throwing gifts at us, small ones and big ones. But often we pick these up and say like the others, "My lucky day," and just walk away. We do not stop to notice the giver; we do not give thanks to God. We are not grateful. And so sometimes we need bricks to fall on us in life to bring us to our senses and raise our minds and hearts to the Divine.

Gratitude, they say, is the memory of the heart. This is why when Jesus gave us the Eucharist, he asked that we celebrate it in memory of him. We remember with gratitude his life, death, and resurrection. Have you noticed that the ones who are naturally grateful in the Gospels are the outcasts? Those condemned by society and religious leaders are often the only ones who are grateful. They remember and relive the power and the presence of the Divine.

People often ask me to give them some simple help to grow in their spiritual life, and I ask them to think about three to five things that happened during their day and be grateful for them as they fall asleep. It is never good to fall asleep thinking about problems or people who upset us or anything negative. These work in our subconscious and will affect us in our waking moments. But if we fall asleep with gratitude on our minds, when we sleep our hearts and our subconscious will continue to look deep for more things to be grateful for.

Gratitude, at its core, is an awareness of gifts and the presence of God. When gratitude becomes our way of life, then we will be praying all the time and always will be happy. This is good for our spiritual, our psychological, and even our physical lives. And with gratitude as our personal attitude, we will be in union with the Divine every moment of our waking and sleeping hours.

26

When You're in Love, You Need Not Know the Purpose of Your Life

I know a good psychiatrist who helped people all his life. He lived a full life and was in his nineties and spent long hours in prayer. One day, he asked God if his life had any purpose anymore. He was losing his hearing and his eyesight, though he still retained his sense of humor and bright spirit. But did his life have any purpose now? He prayed for a long time and waited. And then in the silence of his heart he heard God say to him, "I have a plan for you, but you will not know it. You will fulfill this plan, but will not know it either." He heard this message so clearly that he broke down and wept like a little child. His life even in his nineties did still have a purpose after all. He lived in love with the Divine and God was real to him.

We do not have to be ninety to wonder if our life has any purpose. We all wonder about it from time to time. I guess when our purpose does not seem clear, God could say the same thing he said to this psychiatrist.

I remember a scene in one of Federico Fellini's movies, *La Strada*: The young lady Gelsomina (played by Guilietta Masina) who accompanies Zampanò (played by Anthony Quinn), a street circus performer, is attracted to him. Even though she is ill-treated by Zampanò, she does not abandon him; and he in turn will not let her go, even though she is anything but intelligent. In one of those thought-provoking scenes of Fellini's, Gelsomina asks the clown in the circus if her life has any meaning. The clown answers that everything has meaning. Of course, he does not know *what* meaning anything has—but the clown picks up a pebble and tells her, "This pebble has a purpose or else nothing in life has any meaning or purpose."

This reminds me of the story by Loren Eisley of the little boy on the beach who found thousands of starfish washed ashore early one morning. He began to pick them up lovingly, one by one, and throw them back into the water. An older man watching him was amused and asked him what difference would it make given the thousands of starfish lying on the seashore? He picked up the next starfish, kissed it, and threw it back into the water, saying, "It makes a difference to this one." Often in life we cannot really help the entire world, but if we find our little starfish and help it back to life, our own lives will be worthwhile.

In the Gospels what does Jesus ask people to do? Jesus calls people to be with him and to remain in his love. He does not call us to do great things for him and for God's kingdom. When we spend time just being with God, we will be soaked in God's love and God's life, and this will overflow to others and into the world. This will work its purpose through us, whether we realize it or not. Only then do the great things happen; this is what transforms the world into a heaven on earth. Anything else is merely us "succeeding" in the world, without the power of true transformation.

27

The Goal of Life Is Not to Be a Good Person

When we are in love with the Divine, we realize that the goal of life is not to be a good person. Life is not about being good.

There are many people in this world who are good. But in one sense, they are good for nothing. They are so satisfied, and so happy, and so content with their being good that they have stopped living, stopped growing, and merely exist. They are not part of the dynamic life that keeps moving along and opens up to the deeper experiences. They are like those who speak yesterday's language to tomorrow's people and wonder what is wrong with everyone else. They dream about and live the good old days—which, by the way, are the past and no longer real. They do not have a desire for "the more" of life, for the infinite possibilities. So in one sense, they will never be in love with God, because God is always bigger and deeper, more freeing and more life-giving. The goal of life then is not to be good, it's to become better.

We all hear voices that tell us otherwise: *I am so happy. I go to church every Sunday. I am so active in my parish. I do so many good things. I contribute to so many charities. I am sure I have accumulated much merit in heaven. Why should I change this?* This is good—of course it is good. *And I have this great relationship with God.* Of course that, too, is wonderful. I'm not saying that it isn't. But these voices draw us and lead us nowhere. These voices are not the voice of God. God will destroy this great relationship of ours so that we and the relationship can grow and become even better.

Take the Pharisees in the New Testament. They were good people. They always did what was demanded by the law, were very loyal, and very obedient. They were the really good people—who sat in judgment of everyone else. They did not have an identity of their own except in comparing themselves with the rest of the world. They used their good lives to feel superior to everyone else. They could not think of living outside the parameters of the law, nor could they accept anyone who did. They could not celebrate and enjoy life because of the fear of making mistakes and getting lost.

Or it's like the elder brother in the parable of the prodigal son. A wealthy father has two sons, and the younger son asks to have his share of the estate before his father dies, then leaves home to have a good time with the money, squanders it, and is soon starving and destitute. After much suffering, the younger son finally returns home, penitent of heart. The father welcomes his long-lost son home with great love and rejoicing, and he throws a big feast to celebrate, slaughtering their finest fatted calf. But the older son, who was working out in the field, becomes angry. The elder son says to his father, "All these years I served you and not once did I disobey your orders," and he begrudges his father's celebration at the return of his wayward brother. He refuses to even come into the house. This older son was not ready for the better. He was there staying with the good. And so—being with the good—he wasn't open to a greater love with the father. He wasn't there *with* the father in love; in fact, his own words tell us that he lived not like a son but a servant in his father's house.

Had the elder son been there for the better, he too would have thrown open his arms to welcome back his younger brother. In fact, had he been looking for the better, he too probably would have left home and gone off himself looking for the more, looking for the possibilities. But he was there—the faithful, obedient servant in his father's house. That's the word he uses: "All these years I *served* you and not once did I disobey your orders; yet you never gave me even a young goat to feast on with my friends." He wouldn't know how to celebrate. He was too obedient, too loyal! He would have no time and he would not have known how to cherish life.

The younger son's thirst for the better taught him how to celebrate life, just like his father knew how to celebrate life. Notice that the father did not refuse or go after his son when he left home, but watched him risk everything seeking the fullness of life. The returning younger son is in love with the father and in love with life. The generosity and the expanse of his father's heart he made his own.

The younger son is like Jesus' parable of the one sheep that got lost and earned a celebration from the shepherd. The ninety-nine sheep who were good and would never risk venturing out of the flock to seek the better life, they are like the older son.

Now there are some people who relate to the good older son and think that he has a valid argument when he complains about not being given a kid goat and getting a celebration of his own. These people, like the older son, have turned a deaf ear to the loving father's profound words: *"Everything I have is yours."* This is huge. Everything that the father has is *already* his. This is what the elder son—not being in love—doesn't seem to understand, doesn't seem to recognize or be able to accept. He's not accepting his birthright as the son, as an heir, like St. Paul says: as children of God, we are Divine heirs. So the father's response reminds us of this truth, and also beautifully shows the father's infinite love for the elder son—even at the very moment of his son's bitterness and lack of love.

So the older brother is like many of us: we do good, we never harm anybody, we work hard, we always keep the laws, keep the commandments. But that's not what life is all about. Life is an adventure, life is dynamic, life is a romance. We're not here on this earth to be good, but we have been put here to become better and better. This is what those who are in love with the Divine know and live. Then life becomes an ever-changing dance in which we reach for the better and find, to our surprise, it's always there. There is always more. The Divine energy is never exhausted.

28

How Do You Know When You Have Fallen in Love with God?

How will we know when we have seen the face of God and are in love? To begin with, everybody else will know. It will be revealed in how we respond in our lives.

If I am in love with God, I make St. Paul's experience my own: in God there are no Jews or Gentiles, slave or free, male or female. I no longer look at you as an object to be used or abused, but I look at you as a person who is loved. In other words, I look at you as the breath of God, the image and likeness of God—beautiful and good. Then you will know that I am someone who has fallen in love with God. Or if I treat you badly or I discriminate against you or I am mean to you, then you know that I haven't really seen God and am not really in love with God. Because when we are in love with God, as St. Ignatius will tell us in the Spiritual Exercises, we will experience the power, presence, and essence of the Divine in every creature.

Jesus said God is love, and anyone who lives in God lives in love, and God lives in him. So in such an experience, you and God become one. And then everything reminds you of the Divine. You feel an interconnectedness with the whole of creation and sense the Divine in everything. When God has touched you, not only will everyone else know it, you will know it. You will simply feel different.

Falling in love with God begins with baptism, when the heavens open and God's voice is heard with the same words that were addressed to Jesus: "You are my beloved Son; with you I am well pleased." If we do not hear these words in our hearts, then we are not really baptized. We have merely gone through the ritual. In John's Gospel, we are told that Jesus did not baptize. Later, Paul emphatically proclaims that he is called not to baptize, but to preach the Good News—God loves us totally and unconditionally. To be baptized is not necessarily to become a Christian and is not necessarily to be dunked in holy water, but it is an initiation for any human being into our relationship with the Divine, where we find the ultimate meaning of our lives.

In Greek to be baptized means "to be soaked," "dunked," or "fully drunk." So just as we experience one who is physically drunk, in baptism we experience one who is soaked and drunk with the Divine. When a person has fallen in love, that person and everybody else knows that something has happened. There is a glow on the face, a sparkle in the eyes, and a lightness in the body. This person radiates positive energy all around, affecting people. The world is a better place just because this person is in it.

This person is like Ella, the grasshopper who had a silver flute. Whenever she played the flute, its music brought hope to the depressed, comfort to those in pain, and joy to all around. Ella was in love with life, with itself, and with the Divine. But then one day another grasshopper began to desire the flute and begged for it and pleaded for it, so much so that Ella finally asked what the other was willing to trade for it. "My heart!" was the reply. So Ella accepted the other grasshopper's heart and then gave the silver flute away. Now when the flute was played, the music that came out of it was the same—but the effect was very different. The second grasshopper's music was no longer the expression of freedom that flowed out of love but one that came from discipline and perfection. It did not have the power to move the hearts of others and transform life.

When we have fallen in love with the Divine, we can look into ourselves and find the Divine image alive more and more. It is no longer we who live but the Divine breath that lives more and more in us and through us. Being so in love with the Divine that lives in us, we are able to accept ourselves at the core of our being, with our light and our shadow, with that which is bright and that which is dark, with our strengths and our weaknesses—and we feel good, we feel happy to be ourselves. We don't want to be anybody else.

Beyond the clay and brokenness of human nature, we are still witness to the presence of the Divine. This creates within us a deep sense of acceptance and freedom. There is an expansion within us that brings out more of *us*, because there's an energy that flows through us that never flowed before. Before there were words, but there was no music. When love happens, our words find their symphony.

That love, that Divine energy, is inexhaustible and overflows. It spills out into life and affects the people and things around us. We begin to look at life differently. We begin to look at people differently. We begin to experience everything differently. When we are in love, every action is a loving action. When we have God in our heart, anything that we do is God—everything that we do is God.

29

Lost in the Being and Essence of the Divine

In the East we have different stories of the salt doll. I like the one in which the salt doll encounters the ocean and wants to find out what the ocean is all about. A wave comes up and washes away the feet of the salt doll. And as the salt doll continues to be attracted to the ocean and is lost in this great experience, wave after wave washes away the salt doll until the salt doll becomes one with the ocean itself. It is then that the salt doll finally realizes what the ocean is and also experiences its true identity.

But the salt does not remain in the ocean—it offers itself and its experience to the rest of the world. Salt finds its purpose only when it is mixed in something else. When you put it in some food, you say, "Oh, this is tasty!" You do not see the salt and yet you know it is there from experience. When salt is mixed into water, it dissolves and you have salt water. Salt finds its identity in being a part of something greater, in losing itself in something else. You and I will find our identity when we are lost in God, when we are lost totally in the Divine. Like the Bible tells us: we are the salt of the earth. And that is the consequence of being fully in love with God. Beautiful consequences! But lack of salt also has an effect; if there is no salt in food then that food is bland—and so are our lives when we are not in the Divine.

The Bible teaches us this same profound lesson through the prophet Isaiah, who tells us that God will never forget us because we are carved on the palms of God's hands (Isaiah 49:14–16). We are tattooed onto God in such a way that no one can take us away from God. A tattoo is permanent. That is our identity and the goal of our lives, to realize our identity tattooed on God.

Jesus continues this theme through the symbol of the vine and the branches. He says he wants us to remain in him, and he in us, so that God's life may flow in and through us (John 15). And with this relationship there is nothing that is impossible in our lives. We will bear abundant fruit, revealing God's glory. In what is known as his Prayer for Unity, Jesus makes this union and communion with the Divine the core of his heart's desire. He prays that we may be in God just as he is in God and God is in him (John 17:21).

We need to go into the very being and essence of God. That is where we all have to be. That's where Jesus wants all of us to be. That's where so many mystics and saints are, from so many faith traditions spanning the globe. Commingled, lost in the very being and essence of God—now that's tremendous!

So as lovers of God, and beloved by God, we cannot be satisfied with anything less than the very being and essence of the Divine. This may not be the best way to put it, but I put it this way: If a Christian dies singing, "Jesus is my everything," that is good but disappointing. If a Christian dies singing, "Abba, Father," that is not enough because there is certainly a deeper relationship and experience. If a Christian is lost with the Spirit, that is good—but also not enough. Because the grace available to any person seeking Divine experience is to be lost in the being and essence of God. That is where each person finds their ultimate identity.

And it is a grace. That is to say, it is a gift of God. It cannot be earned or bought or made by our own effort. But it *is* available to us all. Child of God and therefore Divine heir!

When we find ourselves in the being and essence of God, our lives totally change. Once I am commingled with God, I do not see myself as a man. I don't see myself as a priest. I don't see myself as a Jesuit. I don't see myself as a Christian. I see myself as the breath of God. Similarly, I see beyond your being a female or male, beyond your race, your religion, and can look at you as a person. Without effort, I see myself as a person in God, and I see you as a person in God. And there is no greater expression, no greater experience, of being in love with God than that.

Conclusion: The Infinite Possibilities from Being in Love with the Divine

When the Buddha found his enlightenment and realized himself as part of the whole Divine cosmic energy, he exclaimed, "In all the earth *I* alone exist." He had discovered his personal identity in the Divine. Now he had two options. One was to say, "Now that I've found this, I can pass on and ascend into the next life." Or he could say, "I can go back and share this with others." He chose to return to the people and share with them the pathway he had found and make this universal energy available to anyone who sought it. St. Paul, in his letter to the Philippians, says that he struggled between the desire to be with the Divine or to stay with the people to help their salvation. He too made the decision to work with people for their progress and joy in their faith. The Buddha and St. Paul—like Jesus in this sense—came to show us a pathway so that we could live our life most meaningfully and effectively. Through this pathway we would deepen our communion with the Divine and experience what it means to be a Divine heir—life with infinite possibilities and gifts within God.

Whatever our spiritual tradition, or if we are living outside a tradition, we all need to take up the beautiful challenge of walking our path because it's *our own* spiritual journey. No one can walk it for us. Although Jesus or the Buddha, the saints and prophets, gurus and religious leaders of the past or present can point toward a way, only you are able to take the steps day by day to live this. Your own Divine identity is waiting for *you* to claim it, and your personal experience is waiting for *you* to embrace and honor it.

This kind of personal experience and wisdom was paramount for St. Ignatius on his pathway. His experience is like the story of the six blind men and the elephant. Each blind man is feeling some part of this creature, and together they are attempting to discover what it is they are experiencing. One says, "I feel something flat and pliable." The next says, "Whatever I am experiencing is large and impassible, a wall of some kind." Another says, "Well, what I experience is something round, planted to the ground." And so on. Each describes their own unique experience, but all of them are discovering the same elephant. Each of them has only a part of the reality of the whole elephant. Like the six blind men, we need to open ourselves to both the experiences of others and to the greater possibilities in order to get a better and a fuller perspective of reality.

Sometimes we take our experiences and our beliefs and put them into a structure, into a form, and almost choke them. We secure our limited experience in stone and close ourselves to the greater realities of life. Then we are unable to experience the infinite possibilities that exist within God. There's a Buddhist's koan that says, "If you see the Buddha, kill him." Because the last words of the Buddha were, "Be lamps unto yourselves." So wisdom is within you. The only wisdom that will change you is when *you* look into yourself and find the truth and the life within *you*. We really do not believe anything that anyone proclaims—not even if it is written in the Scriptures. But we must check everything against our deep inner experience of our relationship with the Divine and then form and take responsibility for our beliefs. Jesus said the same thing: the kingdom of God is within you. Look inside.

This is what St. Ignatius did; he found his direction and purpose in life within himself rather than looking to external laws or structures. His ever-deepening experience of God formed his guiding truth in life, and everything else was relative to this experience. He says this in no uncertain words in his *Autobiography*, which he left as his testament of the tremendous gifts and graces he had received: "These things he experienced strengthened him then and always gave him such strength in his faith that he has often thought to himself: If there were no Scriptures to teach us these matters of faith, he would be resolved to die for them, solely because of what he has experienced" (*Autobiography*, 29). Ignatius had his fundamental experiences when he spent time in Manresa. They were foundational and in a way formed an absolute criterion for the rest of his life. All else was relative.

When Ignatius wrote the rule of life for anyone following his pathway, he gave us the one law which should direct our lives: More than any exterior rule, the interior law of charity and love, which the Holy Spirit writes and engraves upon hearts, would be the sole guiding principle (*Constitutions*, 134). The interior law will always supersede any exterior law. Living by the supreme wisdom and goodness of God will sometimes take us beyond sacred boundaries, releasing the choke hold that we and outside forces have formed around our relationship with God. And this interior law lives in every person; it is already "engraved" upon our hearts. We only have to listen for and open ourselves to it. This spiritual energy within then inflames us with Divine love that will overflow into all of our life.

By following this supernatural principle, Ignatius can be placed among the sages of ancient times who gave us eternal truths. Already the prophet Jeremiah told us that God could not trust his people with the external laws and an external covenant. He therefore gives them personal experiences where they will not be able to doubt who they are and what God expects of them. They will also find the will and inspiration within their own hearts to live by the inner covenant:

> This is the covenant which I will make with the house
> of Israel after those days, says the LORD. I will place my
> law within them, and write it upon their hearts; I will
> be their God, and they shall be my people. No longer
> will they have need to teach their friends and kinsmen
> how to know the LORD. All, from least to greatest, shall
> know me, says the LORD.
>
> —*Jeremiah 31:33–34*

These words of Jeremiah are reflected in so many of the world's great religious traditions.

And finally we look again to the Buddhist tradition that brings out this principle of interior covenant so beautifully:

> So, Ananda, you must be lamps unto yourselves. Rely on yourselves, and do not be dependent on external help. Hold firm to the truth as a lamp and a refuge, and do not look for refuge in anything besides yourselves. A person becomes his or her own lamp and refuge by continually looking on one's body, feelings, perceptions, moods, and ideas.
>
> *—Digha Nikaya* ii. 99–100,
> "Maha-parinibbana Sutta"

So take courage, and trust in your inner self and your ability to walk your spiritual path. The gift that Jesus offered after his resurrection was, "Peace and courage!" Peace that the world cannot give and an inner bliss that no one and nothing can take away from you. With help from the wisdom of the ages, you can look into yourself and through discerning love discover who you really are and enjoy the infinite possibilities that life holds for you at every step or moment of this Divine encounter.